AF411768

American Mystic

A Journey of Crossing
The Borders of Normal Experience

By William Fitzell

LONE PINE PRESS

New York

...Visits

To

The

Invisible

World

DEDICATED

TO YOUR CROSSING THE BORDERS

THAT LIE BEFORE YOU

ACKNOWLEDGEMENTS

Mom, Dad and Friends, Kindred spirits, living and dead; Robert Wiseman, Professor of Phenomenology and Guide; Robert Creeley, American Poet and Mentor; Those Worthies of Tibetan Mysticism, Govinda, Master Lama and Alexandra David-Neel for their example; Chinese Poets, Li Po, Tu Fu, and Wang Wei, who provide a measure of how far we err; the North American Indians and their Moieties; A host of Mineral, Plant and Animal spirits who frequent the precincts of the Invisible World, and most particularly, a certain Genius Loci, who willynilly cast me out onto the Mystic Path....

I HAIL, SALUTE AND LOVE YOU ALL!

Contents

I

INTRODUCTION

*"A good Booke is the pretious life blood of a mafter fpirit,
imbalm'd and treafurid up on purpofe to a life beyond life"*
- John Milton

1. THE INVISIBLE WORLD

The journey you are about to take is unlike anything you
may have taken. You will cross into another realm of reality and
share in a new way of seeing the world. You will experience what
remains for most, an unknown world, an invisible world. Your
belief system will be tested and many of you will retreat back to
ordinary reality - the defined and visible world - as you understand
it. It's very easy to dismiss miracles or the unfamiliar as fantasy or
pure imagination. You are not alone and share the majority
opinion with everyone.

Notwithstanding, everything you read here is true and
happened in the manner and place described. I have made up
nothing - this is my life. I make no apologies for it. It is a mystic
life as my experiences often describes contact with the spirit world
as well as interactions with an invisible world.

This world is not for everyone. If you are easily upset,
either emotionally or mentally, by events that challenge the logical

or rational explanations that ordinary life offers, then I caution you not to attempt this journey. It is not for you. The world is filled with books for you; but, this is not one of them.

I, myself, have been frightened, upset and even de-stabilized at times by these mystic interventions that occurred with growing regularity from early life into my maturity. For most of my life, I attempted to pass off these events as of little account. I was reinforced in this attitude by everyone around me. I always chose the acceptable explanations for everything and dismissed what remained unexplained. My schooling assisted in this process, from elementary through post graduate study. All this was to change.

What happened to me one summer day was to give the lie to all that I had learned, over a life time of guided instruction. It was a frightening awakening into a new perception of our whole world, that involved a *total shift in consciousness.* A new and extraordinary vision of our world emerged. As most never see it, I call it The Invisible World.

To see what can't be seen, hear what can't be heard, know what can't be known, this is what I'm talking about. Deeply moved and scared out of my wits, I was not prepared for this assault on my sanity. My head swelled up, my eyes watered, my hands shook, my heart pounded for days after this new vision of our world. I told no one for a long time, until I could calm myself, and accept what now became my secret vision. I feared someone would look into my eyes, and see what I had seen and experienced; so I continued to avoid people for awhile, by living alone in the Sierra foothills, until I could discover what had happened to me.

I slowly came to realize that I could not have received this mystic vision on my own: I had been given some special help from somewhere, outside myself. I am not unduly religious, nor do I meditate, have a Guru, or take drugs. Books were of little help, except to recall that sometimes people had had visions, while starving or meditating on some mountain top. I knew that what happened to me was different.

So I begin my journey at the end, for only so, was I armed with the perception to see what had come before....what I had not seen over a lifetime. Accept with an open mind and ···· stalwart heart this true account of my life. It is my highest hope this journey of mine will help others and illuminate the way.

* * * * * * * * *

PART II

CROSSING OVER

"All this visible world is but an imperceptible point in the ample bosom of nature."

- Pensées, Pascal

2. GENIUS LOCI: ENTERING THE WATER WORLD

We all live on a water planet. Someone once said that man himself is, "a walking bag of sea water." All of us sense an affinity and an attraction toward streams, lakes and the ocean. Water seems to relax us and tug at something within our essential selves, pulling us toward our primal world. Inland cities sport bubbling fountains to remind us of our remote past.

* * * * * * * * *

After heavy March rains, I was repairing a damaged spillway out of my pond. The rocks had been pushed aside and down the stream. I set about replacing them atop the spillway to slow down the outflow of the pond. The water continued to rush through the rocks, this is to say, around the rocks, making what we would call a rushing water sound of gurgling, watery echoes.

When I suddenly heard a new and unfamiliar noise joining the other sounds, I was surprised; it was much louder and drowned out the earlier rushing sounds, as almost groans, arose from the water. Its eerie, high, hollow note was hard to describe in words.

I thought of water singing, as it hit those rocks and gushed through the openings it found between and around them. It was Nature singing its own song. Unwittingly, I had played a role by my moving the rocks, gushing sounds reemerged, of a typical rush of water over rocks. There is more to this than I had realized. There is something about water that we do not perceive. What was its true essence? What don't we understand about it?

I thought of the Japanese who have developed rock-in-stream arrangements for centuries, making it an art form. They often spend years trying to capture certain water sounds, songs. The Balinese people have used water sounds to judge the outflows into their irrigated fields and do so to this day.

The North American Indians paid homage to the water spirits as the Thai people of today celebrate water spirits in their annual festivals. But as to the exact nature of a water spirit, I had not an idea. It remains for most of us today, a fanciful myth.

* * * * * * * * *

Knowing all this, I was unprepared for what happened to me one remarkable day. It was to alter my relationship with water and how I saw the world...forever.

A hot summer day sent me down to Perry Creek to cool off. I was sitting by an old mining dam in the Sierra foothills. The dam is only ten feet falling across and creates a waterfall of some six or eight feet, into a deep pool at its base. It is a place of great natural beauty, where birds and animals are drawn to its falling water, gushing into the pool below. It is cool and mossy with ferns growing around a pool, sunk into hard granite rocks. Giant Oak and Willow trees line the small canyon on either side -- mountain lions come to drink from this stream and tiny hummingbirds nest in branches over the rushing stream below. Clearly, it is a special and unusual place. Indian grinding stones line parts of the surrounding plateaus above this stream, where Maidu Indians camped in centuries past.

I was totally relaxed in this naturally beautiful environment, listening to the water and the birds and watching an occasional lizard basking in the sun. I expected nothing out of the ordinary.

21

SUDDENLY I FOUND MYSELF BECOME WATER, I WAS ONE WITH THE WATER. That is the only way I can clearly describe what happened to me. I merged with the water in the pool. I was totally disembodied from myself -- I left my body behind. I observed I had become within an instant, without any thoughts about it, indeed without any preparation at all - WATER.

I felt cool and vibrant being water. As I swirled under the waterfall, the light SPARKLED all around me, as it reflected off the rocks in the channel holding me.

Still, I was frightened out of my wits. I feared that the water had possessed me without my leave. A reassurance, a guiding voice, a light sense calmed my fears: *It was alright to be water.* Even though, I still had trouble with it, I no longer panicked. I seemed to be the eyes and ears of the water and helped water to see itself, joining my consciousness with water. I felt it wanted me to do this, so I was willing to let this happen.

I was being controlled by a force that overwhelmed my mind with a greater consciousness. The reassurance feeling returned. *I was alright and should not be frightened.* Still, it was very hard not to enjoy my new state of consciousness. I let go of the nagging doubts my mind presented. It was a triumph, for a sense of freedom filled me. *I could just be.*

No longer me, the body...now me, the water, flowing across the land. The sun glistened and warmed my surface water, while

I remained cool. I was very conscious of movement, of flow, of wet rocks around me. I smelt the damp mosses, lining the walls of the channel through which I moved. What most interested me was the light, or rather dancing lights, reflecting off of everything around me and even through me. Waves of light bounced around me, and I bounced with it. This turmoil of distracted light was so incredibly beautiful and thrilling; consciousness of sounds of splashing water, gurgling and rushing, *filled me with bliss.* Then I was sucked out into a stream, into a distant horizon of pure overwhelming energy. All was oneness now.

My consciousness remained in this suspended state. I began to wonder if I was dead -- all seemed still and calm now after the turbulence of moving water. My mind began to question my new state of *being water* - it was fulfilling and complete yet, a shift in my consciousness occurred...thinking...I was me, the body...again. My consciousness re-inhabited its former home...my body.

As unexpectedly as I became water, I had become Bill Fitzell again, sitting in my chair, dry and warm, gazing at the water below. I was as amazed at this feat, as I had been at my first change. I was in body again. I was back as myself, as spontaneously as I had left my body as it sat under a Willow tree.

I immediately questioned what had happened to me and the frightening thoughts returned. I had not been prepared for this experience by anything in my life.

The power of this water to take me into it -- possess me, now frightened me. What if I didn't want to be water? Did it care? Was it more powerful? What force could so possess me? Was it even possible that this had happened to me at all? Did I imagine this? No! I did not imagine all this. The water did it, overpowered me. Some extraordinary power caused or performed this miracle on me. I realized that to imagine something from your familiar state of consciousness, you have to believe that it is even possible. To me, this was not a thing possible to do. (It was impossible). Yet, it had happened spontaneously.

I came to believe that things that we consider inanimate do indeed possess consciousness and powers that we are not aware they have. The line between living and nonliving is an illusion. I had crossed this border between living and nonliving, however briefly.

The more I thought about what had happened to me, the more I came to the conclusion, I had experienced a force in nature that transcends all forms; a life force, a spirit that supersedes all, that posses all. It may be as basic as an all-encompassing energy field, that we rarely are aware enough to experience, that lies all around us unseen.

Our thoughts focus on the materials that surround us and we don't see the process, the energy, that pervades every material thing. However, if we are calm and accepting of our surroundings, then it is possible that a certain GENIUS LOCI may allow us an extraordinary vision of the underlying reality that surrounds us and of which we are an inseparable part. It is rare; but no less real. I came to realize that a certain GENIUS LOCI had grasped me and threw me into an invisible world, of which I knew nothing, not even of its existence. How many more spirits, animals and plants lay about us I wondered, what a slow study I was. I don't believe I could have experienced this transcendental event without the help of this spirit, or guardian, or helper of travelers, who would cross the greatest divide, between the temporal and the eternal: our bodies and the timeless water of which we are part...our atoms reassemble to pass again...now water, now human, later something yet again.

As the weeks passed, so did my fears of what had happened to me; I saw it as a great awakening. I determined that my life had undergone a series of what I now saw as mystical events. I would write an account later of these, starting with early childhood up to the present (some fifty years). There seemed to be a pattern: From the earliest recollection of being washed by my mother, when I was but two years old and actually observing how my skin glistened, up to those events of a decidedly more mystical nature as I grew up in New England and there were many.

I would focus on those that were somehow beyond ordinary happenstance, that pointed to something beyond our own world and our understanding of it, to an invisible, unseen world. I discovered that animals have played a significant role throughout my life and indeed have saved my life on occasion - yet, I had earlier dismissed this from my conscious recollection. I would now acknowledge their help, guidance and protection. Where would I be without their timely intervention? Dead most assuredly!

I would start my account as a child...

* * * * * * * * *

"Never does Nature say one thing and wisdom another."

- Juvenal

3. THE BOY AND THE BEAR

A hot New Hampshire summer day found me wandering away from the farm house into the forest. It was cool and fresh after crossing the open fields. An eight-year-old boy thinks little of getting lost; so I gleefully escaped from the clutches of an overprotective aunt and kind and generous grandmother, who had charge of me that summer.

Cascades of water echoed from a nearby stream hidden from my view by towering ferns. Half crawling on all fours, I soon discovered the water rushing over rocks into pools, along the mossy banks of a fast moving stream. I marveled at its life and force, as it rushed through the openings between boulders and fallen tree trunks.

My boyhood senses took it all in -- the pine-scented air, the buzzing insects, the sunlight through the tree tops, the coolness on my skin. What a great delight it was to discover myself in such a place. This would be my secret retreat -- that only I knew about. I claimed it as my own when suddenly...

I saw his eyes looking at me...Gulp!...Out of nowhere, a huge black bear loomed up and swayed before me on the path; my heart almost stopped beating. Scared out of my wits at this sudden encounter, this unexpected threat -I turned and ran for my life, half crying with shock and fear. I became entangled in brush and vines but continued to escape, as the bear moved toward me. I could now see only *black fur moving in the bushes* -- no head, eyes, nose, teeth -- *just fur.* I had touched it. He seemed to be everywhere at once, as I turned around to the left, he appeared to head me off; I'd turn to the right and there he was again, cutting me off - I was terrified at my inability to get past him and backed up against a tree - numb with fear. It was then, when I stopped trying to get round him, that I no longer saw him. I retreated backwards. I jumped over rocks and trees in my panic. I remember yelling like hell, "HELP!" Soon I emerged out into the open pasture and could see the farmhouse nearby. Still running, my heart throbbing with fear, I crossed the field into the farmyard, then to the house. Pushing open the screen door, I entered the safety of the kitchen.

My throat was dry and gravelly as I gasped.

Then a rush of barely intelligible words streamed out of my mouth. I told of my near-death experience, of nearly being eaten alive by a great black bear. Grandma "Bommy" hugged me against her apron, while Aunt Katherine fished out some freshly baked cookies for me, by way of distraction. As I munched away, she warned me against ever again wandering into the woods like that, and to stay close to the house in the future.

All the rest of the summer, I never lost sight of the farmhouse -- having learned my lesson -- *the woods are dangerous.* Yet, the farmhouse yard proved to be not safe either, as I was bitten by a large beetle while sitting under a tree; the sting hurt for days and proved to be more hurtful than being scared. At least the bear didn't bite me when I had touched him. The kids back home on Dixie Ave. would never believe me, Grandma didn't.

Now, years later, in thinking about the bear encounter, I realized that the bear actually saved me from having wandered too far into the forest and getting lost. This could have been my real danger, although at the time, I never realized it. How blind I was, or more specifically - how unconscious I was, for in a very real sense, the bear was a blessing in disguise, my guardian in the woods. It was not so much as an escape as a rescue; more it was a meeting with Nature's wildness, for which I was unprepared.

This, as it would turn out, was to be but the first of many encounters with the stewards of nature, its animal and spirit forces.

There would be others. Often what appears to be a threat or risk is proven afterward to be a help to us. It certainly was so, as far as I could ascertain, in looking back now with hindsight.

A few years later, I was to really experience a close call, which strangely had all but vanished from my recollection in later life. My water consciousness had awakened me to a whole new perception of my life. Where I would have been without this wake-up call -- I hesitate to say -- Asleep no doubt.

* * * * * * * * *

"Innumerable twinkling of the waves of the sea."

Aeschylus, 456 B.C.

4. MIRACLE AT DUCK ISLAND

A blue kayak had washed up on the beach. The frame was somewhat damaged, but the canvas hull was not torn up. I set about repairing it, with twine and some patching and soon it was seaworthy. I was fourteen and my brother, eleven. We had never had our own boat. This was a thrilling find, a giant leap from our old raft of the previous summer. We counted ourselves sailors, for we had experience taking the raft out, beyond the breaking waves and along the shoreline the whole of last summer.

We became explorers of the many island creeks and marshes around the state park at Hammonasset in Connecticut. We spent idyllic days crabbing for blues or fiddlers. Soon we hankered for a real adventure.

The Gull and Duck Islands, actually large rocks, out in Long Island Sound soon beckoned. One morning, we set out paddling toward the islands. Taking turns to pace ourselves, we fairly flew through a light choppy sea and made rapid progress. Seagulls flew overhead, squawking at our assault on their islands. Within a few hours, we made our final approach. Our kayak skimmed through the channel that divided the islands. We felt the currents quicken as we approached our destination. We would be glad to finally climb out of our cramped canvas boat onto the solid huge rock after a few scary misses. We tied the boat up and sat down to have the light lunch we carried.

Water churned and waves sent up a constant spray of water. All around us screeching gulls circled overhead disturbed by our intrusion on their island. We were tired but happy. We downed our peanut butter and jelly sandwiches and apples. What an adventure! Here we were, totally alone. The lapping waves shimmered around us and the smell of the sea delighted our senses. All was wonderful to our inexperienced eyes.

We rested atop the rocks and talked about our conquest and how envious the kids back at the campground would be. "One Arm" Johnny would never believe we came out here. A victim of polio, his crippled arm forbade such adventures.

The distant shoreline seemed hazy in the afternoon sun. Then with somewhat of a jolt, we realized how far we had come in our small kayak, and how far it would be to get back. Maybe we had come too far?

It was already getting late and we had to start back. Mother would be wondering where we were by now. We hurriedly re-boarded our shaky craft and headed back through the channel, between the two islands toward the shoreline. It wasn't too long before I noticed that the current was running against us and out toward sea. Paddling was very hard and tiresome. The lightness of the boat was also cause for concern. The currents easily pushed it around in direction and toward the sea.

Then it slowly hit me --the tide had turned, and was now going out to sea. After floundering around with little or no progress toward the channel, I knew we were in serious trouble. The sun, too, was sinking and daylight would soon disappear. "Oh we should never have come out here!," my brother fearfully cried out.

Our craft continued to be buffeted by the quickening tide and we could barely hold our own with our steady paddling. Overhead, the gulls screeched at us and all seemed turmoil, the possibility of drowning now appeared a likely outcome to all this. The sharp piercing calls of the birds echoed in my head and somehow quickened my awareness. We were now in a new and strange environment, where life and death cross paths. Could we hold to the life path? The fear of death gripped our hearts and squeezed and tested our resolve. The choppy sea roiled about us and occasionally sprayed our faces with its force.

Deep blue green water swirled and rippled below us. Our own hearts seemed to sink, still we paddled with all our might. We called out -- our cry to survive -- deep within ourselves.

Then it happened. SOMETHING HAD NUDGED THE BOAT. I felt a push, then another, then another. What on earth (or sea) is happening? Shock and disbelief confronted us -- now what?. Sharks? No! The boat was being *pushed* steadily -- even *uplifted* -- *carried* by something underneath the boat -- toward shore and the coastline. We tried to figure out what...Then the canvas bottom of the boat *bulged up under us* and I looked into the water. Giant fish? No. Porpoises were the only answer. Yes, large shapes moved all around our boat, nudging us along before them. Amazed, I couldn't paddle, but I didn't need to, as we moved out of the channel and continued toward shore. We were speechless, held by some great sense of relief and gratitude to these sea creatures who had saved us. Our relief overcame our wonder, at what was happening to us. The unbelievable became natural and we accepted it, without question, now as it was, because it was. THE PORPOISES WERE HELPING US. Why they should help us was beyond our understanding. Had this ever happened to anyone before? We hadn't a clue. No one would believe us, if we told it to anyone.

We came closer to shore now, the current running against us lessened. The porpoises were gone just as quickly as they had appeared. I paddled and headed toward the breakers. Paddling toward them, we could see a small group of people on the shore. As we came closer, I saw mother and a Park Ranger among them. We pulled up on shore. A small group walked toward us. We were very scared; we knew they had been looking for us. Mother asked where we had gone. I pointed toward the islands in the distance, but there were none to be seen in the dying light over the Sound. So I said, as I jumped up and down in relief, "The Islands." Mother thanked the Ranger and took us back to the campground. She said she had been worried all day about us and would tell father. We knew what this meant. She also forbade us from using the kayak for the rest of the summer and fed us no supper that night.

My younger sister later asked, "Why did you dance up and down after getting out of the boat?" I could only answer that "I was happy to be back on shore." I was happy to be alive; my jumping up and down was an unconscious reaction to my aliveness and joy at being saved by the porpoises.

With all the ensuing punishments, we forgot THE MIRACLE we had experienced and never mentioned it to anyone. We feared they would think we were crazy. We had been crazy enough, to have ever ventured out to the islands in the first place.

Years later, we were to realize that without the adventure, the risk we took, we would never have experienced the miracle. Yet, the questions remain until this day, Why?, How?

Often it takes a crisis, or an overwhelming need, to make the break -- out from the normal everyday acceptance of what is presented to us at the time. "Don't go into the woods...," "Stay on the shore where it is safe," "Don't take risks," these become the easy solutions to life's challenges. So our life is limited, as well as its potential for growth and joy. Children are specially easy to condition, but our greatest responsibility is to live life to its fullest. How many of us pass that test?

Yet, the risk should never be ignored as it is a real one.

The following year our neighbors had gone fishing, off Duck Island, in their small power boat. All were lost, assumed to have drowned, as the boat was never found. Perhaps in their heavy wooden boat, the porpoises couldn't help them; perhaps they didn't call out for help, deep within themselves, as we had done.

Two rescues now, one by the sea creatures we know as porpoises and the earlier one, by a black bear. "What next?", I asked myself, as I reviewed my life journey, until now so little understood. Tears of gratitude now filled my eyes as my mind wandered back along the track of time...discovering...what so often had been denied...the Wonders, the Joy...that was suppressed in my life, and made colorless.

* * * * * * * * *

"Thence we came forthe to see the stars again."

- Dante

5. QUEEN MARY'S DELIVERANCE

The grand ocean liner glided down the Hudson River, past the towering skyscrapers of lower Manhattan, and out to sea. It was all behind me now -- a broken engagement, the pleadings of father, "to be responsible," the offers at the bank, of "higher wages." Yet, I knew in my gut, it was time to get on with my life and a sense of giddy relief overwhelmed me at my new found freedom and possibilities. I had a six-month vacation staring me in the face. The price was to disappoint everyone, hopeful of my Wall Street career: a small price to pay for freedom. The mid 1960's was a time for taking chances, an age of experimentation.

Those early days were idyllic, the Queen was made for sailing. Her wood fittings creaked gently, as she plowed through the furrows of each oncoming wave. The midnight buffet on deck, the beef tea each morning as the steward tucked me into my deck chair, piled with blankets against the bracing ocean breezes, the high tea each afternoon, with trays piled high with cakes, biscuits, cookies and tiny finger sandwiches, was all too delightful.

Everything seemed perfect, feasting all day and dancing all night. Then one evening, while "twisting the night away," I became overheated and decided to cool off with a walk around the deck. The ocean fairly sparkled, under a full moon, as I gazed over the rail. I saw a distant ship passing back toward America, its lights beaming brightly. Stars shown overhead in a clear sky. Then, out of the corner of my eye, I saw movement. Turning toward the fantail of the ship, I noticed someone moving about -- no, throwing something overboard. Intrigued, I moved closer to better discover what it was. A young woman of twenty or so, in a party dress, was casting things into the swirling ocean below her. Then, I saw it was her clothing, piece by piece, that went over the rail. Impelled to intervene, I walked up to her and asked her why she was throwing her clothes overboard.

A long minute passed before she answered that, "Had no one seen me, I would have thrown myself in, as well as my clothes." She truly wanted to end her life. I responded, "It's a dramatic way to go, but wasn't life meant to be lived?" After a few moments, she very reluctantly agreed that, "perhaps you are right."

I suggested a drink in the Starlight Lounge, which she accepted. Together, we left the fantail and entered the lounge where the band played on. We had a drink then danced the night away. No more was said about her suicide attempt.

I presumed that her impulse or desire to end it all, had passed. She appeared happy and vital by the time we parted. What a lucky event, to have saved the life of a pretty young girl, just starting out in life. My getting overheated lead to our connection that pulled her back from the brink of oblivion toward the dance of life. Or was it something else? (Some unheard cry of the human soul). (Somehow or way, I was propelled to make that fateful interception and a life was saved). Had I been like a porpoise nudging her back to life's shore?

What if I had not found her in time? I'll never know. Some all-powerful force lies just below our waking consciousness, ready and willing to make itself known -- if we would listen and heed its message.

Later, I met a couple in their late sixties. They shared our dinner table. The wife exclaimed one evening, "How I envy you young people, going to Europe. John and I are on our first trip to Europe, and I fear it is already too late for us to really enjoy ourselves as you will."

I asked, "But why didn't you go sooner?" in a sympathetic tone.

"Well, we never had the time, what with the children, and John working," she answered, "Oh, I see..." was my response. I had heard it all before. Reasons given and commitments to others, for not fulfilling oneself, for not living. We must do better than that!

The harbor at Cherbourg, France was a jumble of activity, as tow boats assisted in our docking. The hillsides were covered with little houses with hundreds of people cheering and waving to welcome us ashore. They waved the tricolor flags in a genuine joy at our arrival, that I shall never forget. It signaled crossing the finish line, in a symbolic way, a victory of sorts, in the race for life. We had won.

As the boat train left the station for Paris, I thought about the people who never make it across these symbolic finish lines in life. Held back by various injunctions, to be responsible and adhere to the tried and true. Many are engulfed in a sea of ordinary happenstance and talk of "going fishing" when they retire or traveling, but never quite make it, except in their dreams.

As luck or fate would have it, I had found deliverance. What a refinement from the small canvas boat, that almost cost me my life. It seemed that the pattern of my life was one of escapes and crossings, for only so could I put myself in the way of changing and accepting new ways.

After a six month sojourn in Europe, I returned to America and settled on the West Coast, after crossing the Continent. A sense of freedom and joy accompanied me. I began to explore the great stands of Redwood forest and towering mountains of California, much like John Muir before me. I seemed to become more alive; as I opened myself to the natural wonders spread out before me.

* * * * * * * * *

PART III

THE BOUNDARIES OF NATURE

"We carry within us the wonders we seek without us."

- **Sir Thomas Browne**

6. RETURN TO THE FOREST

The Redwood trees of California preserve a sense of the past. Wandering in their cool atmosphere one is in the presence of ferns, mosses, bark, sorrel, and a pervading silence. You are in a different place, where new conditions prevail.

As I walked into this stand of towering huge trees, I sensed I was opening up to their presence and becoming one with the spirit of the place. A heavy scent of pine acted as an inducement, to absorb the energy, that I sensed all around me. Something was different on this visit to Muir Woods. I felt giddy and somehow moved by this energy.

In an intuitive moment of pure love, I threw my arms around a tree and squeezed; slowly I entered into the spirit of the place. The surroundings opened up to me, as my powers of interaction opened to receive this communion. *My sense of self began to dissolve* into my surroundings and a sense of oneness overwhelmed me. I welcomed this new consciousness as it unfolded, and let my old self fade out completely without reservation. A new experience awaited me...A metaphysical union flowed into what used to be me...for me, I no longer was...consciousness I was now. The experience was that I didn't just see trees, moss, rocks and streams anymore -- I became trees, rocks, ground and sensed their energy for the first time. I had always accepted without question their mere appearance as material things, which made me believe, or think, that I was separate from them. The "I", who merely observed them, I now saw as an illusion.   There was no separation. The observer "I" became the observed - trees, rocks...

I was no longer apart from them -- I was one with them and could feel as they felt -- indeed, I shared their consciousness and *felt their bliss at being alive* (energized). It was unrestrained freedom, something I had never experienced or even imagined in my entire life. *It was blissful realization* -- isolation had been vanquished -- tears welled up and flowed in the total release I felt. As I moved through the trees, I felt as if I were in some primeval Garden of Eden, where everything is good and caring. I felt the overwhelming love of creation that pervaded all living things. THE VERY ATMOSPHERE WAS CHARGED WITH LOVE. Love energized everything. A super charge of positive energy fulfilled me.

The atmosphere continued to embrace me and became me and I, it. Boundaries disappeared, melting into an illusionary past. My breathing became like my environment, a low and constant vibration, in total harmony with my surroundings, my extended self.

Words and thoughts about what I was experiencing were useless, and even worse, a distraction from pure being, a blocking of true realization. I allowed thoughts to evaporate, into the irrelevance they so justly deserved and fully savored the feast of life, suffused with loving energy, which I can only call love for all living things.

Fading in and out of body consciousness, I noted trees separate again. The trees around me emitted a low vibration, I could hear, as I moved past each one. The sound was consistent and without variation, like a humming in my ears. Then the unbelievable -- *a laughing dog* appeared in the woods before me. This was not shocking, as I realized it was just a local black dog, who I could now understand to be laughing. Ordinarily, I could only sense a dog's contentment, but here and now I could sense its laughter, and I quickly joined in at its good humor. *Total communication* was possible between us, *without talking or barking.* I seemed to be in his head and he in mine; so, communication of any other kind seemed unnecessary.

His Black hairy body bristled with joy, as I sat down and produced some cheese and bread, which we then shared as equals.

We ate with relish and total enjoyment. He then smiled at me, at my being able to understand him totally, perhaps the only time in his life this happened. Then he disappeared back into the underbrush.

A hummingbird appeared before me, suspended in flight, fixed before my face for some time before flying off again. "Who was observing who?" I asked myself.

Then I heard a strange sound -- breaking my mood -- a shrill, high-pitched growl. Only then did I see a grey fox, peering out at me from atop a large flat rock. I stared at it, and it stared back, before it once again began howling at me. What did it want? Oh, I realized -- I was in its space. I slowly backed away.

I walked along a stream and out of the grove. Coming to a road winding through the entrance, I broke into laughter at this human imposition on Nature. A cement construct, this road was a cosmic joke to me in my heightened state of awareness. Along the road came a large car with two older couples out to see Nature. My laughter became uncontrolled at this further joke -- they were seeing nature out of the windows of a machine. How detached and isolated they appeared to me -- how unknowing of what it all was, and what it all meant. As the car slowly drove away and disappeared, my laughter suddenly stopped. I could see a dead salamander in the road, crushed by their passing wheels. The joke had become a tragedy.

* * * * * * * * *

Although I accumulated a wide circle of friends, at this time of my life, I was always happier when I was alone; for it gave me a chance to become better acquainted with myself. I preferred to live apart, in the mountains, in isolated small villages, or beach communities. I became my own best friend and chose dead poets, philosophers and writers as my companions of the month or day. Occasionally an animal or bird would befriend me and that, too was often enough. I must acknowledge that a reclusive life has its strong points. It was during one of these periods in my life, that the line between living and dead was challenged for the first time.

* * * * * * * * *

- St. Augustine

7. NETHERWORLD

Agate Beach is a small enclave on the coast near Bolinas, California. It is so small, that it does not appear on the map, and no road signs designate its location. It is a remote bird and marine sanctuary on the western edge of the North American continent.

While living in a house overlooking Duxbury Reef, a part of Agate Beach, I came to notice a strange-looking, homeless young man, of thirty or so. Dressed in rags, he had rotten teeth and straggly, long hair. Whenever I encountered him, he was cheerful and friendly. I often noticed him wandering on the ridge, overlooking the ocean, or out around the tide pools, that appear at low tide. No mere solitary wanderer, he appeared to be living in this environment.

He was the ultimate loner, totally alone, and friendless, living in a harsh marginal zone, between ocean and the land. The area was hauntingly bleak, where the ocean waves scoured the sandy cliffs and allowed only a few trees to grow, with lowered branches hugging the ridge line.

When the tide was low, the shore revealed tide pools. It was a marine world, teeming with sea life. Shellfish, crabs, and sea urchins lived in the shallow pools, carved out by the crashing surf. The winds here blow incessantly and loosen pebbles and rocks, forming showers of falling pebbles, amidst the sounds of breaking waves.

How anyone could live in this harsh place was a mystery. I wished to know more. I learned his name from the townspeople in Bolinas. It was Andy. He had been a "fixture" in the town, before coming out to Agate Beach. He had found his niche in this harsh environment.

One day while walking around the Bluff, overlooking the ocean, I came upon a rough hovel -- or what could be better described, as a ditch of some eight or ten feet, covered over with driftwood and scraps of plastic sheeting. Curious, I looked inside and found heaps of old rags and torn blankets, lining the ditch. Nearby were rows and rows of marine skeletons of various fish, crabs, and even birds and small animals.

Feeling I had intruded on what was obviously Andy's abode, I hastily withdrew, and resumed my walk back along the beach. Occasionally, I would see Andy going through my garbage can or those of my neighbors. Every so often he would frighten a child, into crying as he entered someone's yard, or disturb some sleeping dog, into barking at him; yet, the neighbors accepted him. He was harmless, even friendly, if you stopped to talk to him.

Being his closest neighbor, I became his supplier of drinking water, as I discovered when I heard my garden hose running at odd times of the day. I indulged him. In general, he was well liked, as Bolinas is known for being tolerant of different life styles no matter how eccentric. One local tells how a resident purchased a chicken to get the skin, to make a hat for himself and then threw away the bird.

The rumor around town, was that Andy came from a small town in the Midwest, years back, and that his family was wealthy. He dropped out and rejected such privileges, preferring a pure life, unfettered by material concerns. For this, he was greatly respected in the community. It was said that a sister, two years ago, came looking for him, to fetch him back to a "normal life," but failed to achieve her mission and returned after a week of trying.

One day, driving the local coastal hills, I passed Andy along the roadside. He was pushing a shopping cart along the highway, piled high with what had obviously been the reapings of a productive day, over in Mill Valley.

At the time, I was studying piano with my girlfriend, a Julliard School drop-out. We played Bach and Mozart at all hours.   Whenever I met Andy, he would playfully call me "Mozart"; I would laugh at his joke, not realizing he didn't know my name, or why he had made this up. Why not? OK, I'll be Mozart for him. It was his way of relating to me, after all; whenever he came around the house, he heard music.

One day, I offered some old clothes to Andy. To my surprise he declined, preferring the old torn rags he was accustomed to. Now I wondered, is this some pride of his, or an affection to be poor? A sense of integrity? (I was never to find out).

Andy disappeared, his body was never found. His old surfboard was discovered one day on the beach. It was chewed apart on one side. We supposed he had gone out on the surfboard, toward Duxbury Reef. Since the waters near the reef are infested with sharks, all felt he probably was attacked and devoured.

One town wag, suggested that Andy had tried to paddle down the coast, to San Francisco, to get his teeth fixed by a dentist. Anyway, the town turned out for a huge bonfire of driftwood on Agate Beach in his honor - to give him a good send off into the next life. A local feast of shellfish and corn, made it a celebration to remember him by, around the fire that night. He had originally been a local oddity, a curiosity and in the end, he came to be loved by his adopted town.

Several months later, I awoke in the middle of the night. I sat up in my bed, wondering what had disturbed me, as I am a sound sleeper, and usually sleep well into the daylight hours. Alone in the house, I could hear nothing. All was quiet, a total absence of sound in total darkness, a shroud of utter stillness prevailed.

Then, I heard *strange music* being played outside my isolated house. Incredible as this was, this music was unlike any music I ever heard before, or since.

The notes of music came wafting through the night air, at very precise intervals, with an uncanny exactitude - woodwind but without Mozart's touch. Indeed the spaces between one note and the next, were remarkable to hear. The *silences*, rather than the notes, were what struck me with their seemingly *unworldliness.* It was thrilling and indescribable to NOT HEAR, AND HEAR, at the same time. The sounds were flute like, of a high frequency and very pleasing. The high pitch created a profound sense of awe, against the deep silence of the night...yet indescribable...

This eerie concert continued for some time, I delighted in the purity of it. It was a gift of music, or sound, or HEARING WHAT CAN'T BE HEARD. An unheard concert that I somehow heard, this is the only way I can describe it. The irony here is that I'm caught trying to describe non-sound, an impossible task.

Just as mysteriously as it started, it stopped. All was quiet again, except the faint sound of distant waves on the shore. *I realized that Andy had returned for one final visit.* Knowing that I loved music, he visited in a musical form, that was altogether his alone. He made a gift of his music; he played for me something he thought I would enjoy. I did and have never heard anything like it again: that is, not heard the non-heard again.

It's perhaps a toss up as to which I prefer, the ocean or the mountains, for I love them both. I spent the following years traveling to Hawaii and the Sierra Nevada mountains, whenever I could get away from house-building or remodeling old Victorian mansions in San Francisco.

I seemed to develop an empathy with nature, which most would call eccentric, or even weird. I make no defense for myself. I truly enjoyed wilderness and the back country, spending weeks alone, in remote mountain areas, with all the isolation that state affords, perhaps sometimes I went too far.

* * * * * * * * *

"Hi! Ni! Ya! Behold the man of flint. That's me! Four lightning zigzag fromme strike and return."

- Chant, Navaho

8. MOONSTRUCK

Poets have always been fascinated by the moon. To the artist, it became a symbol for the imagination and the nonrational side of man. Luna (moon) became lunatic, or crazy one. It represents freedom from reason and the ability to create and express oneself, without hinderance. Soon the moon itself came to represent the imaginary world of the poet, the opposite of reason, which was symbolized by the sun and its excesses.

But, I ask, isn't the moon more than a symbol? Doesn't it have a power unto itself? What is this power and how does it make itself known? Strange, arcane questions, rarely asked, and never answered.

I had, like most people, regarded the moon as something very beautiful in the night sky. Its monthly phases, into new and full moon, were indeed something poets loved to celebrate. But its effects on me personally, were never fully understood, or even an object of curiosity to me. This, too, was to change, unexpectedly.

One night while on a camping trip, I set up my tent on a bluff, overlooking the Pacific Ocean at Mendocino, California. Being tired, I quickly went to sleep, accompanied by the sounds of

the surf below the cliff, it seemed all I could have expected, or hoped for.

In the middle of the night, the moon awakened me. Somewhat annoyed, I fought to regain my sleep, when the light entered my tent, and seemed to call me to arise and emerge out of the tent. Questioning my sanity, I sleepily crawled outside to witness a huge orb facing me, across the wide Pacific Ocean. It was very large and dominated the sky. Its shining presence dominated the night.

Everything was bathed in a luminous light, pine trees, rocks, every leaf on every branch, every wave and ripple on the shining ocean. How did I think I could escape being shined on, I asked myself? OK, I could accept that in principle, I was no exception and stood muster with the elements around me.

All was saturated with a dazzling show of pure light. The aliveness of the scene before me, quickly overwhelmed me. I felt my senses aroused and quickened, *even struck by the moon's power* over me. It gave out an energy, on some level I could not understand. Some exchange was taking place. I stood a reluctant recruit, on the bluff awaiting orders. It demanded awareness, and sharing.

I gazed at the rising moon for some time and shared its nightly pass overhead, as it diffused its energy, light, and joy. I felt very, very happy and fulfilled in a strange and *preternatural way.* I don't remember climbing back into the tent or sleeping that night. It left me with a heightened awareness, as it tapped my consciousness and altered its knowing.

Some years later, I was backpacking in the High Sierras and had pitched my tent near a mountain stream. Again, in the middle of the night, the moon found me and awoke me with its glaring light. This time, the granite surfaces of huge boulders on both sides of a narrow canyon, reflected and concentrated the moonbeams; so, that the reflected light penetrated underneath the pine trees' cover, lightening up the ground around my tent.

The night air appeared charged, by this unexpected light, and caused my skin to tickle, and my hair to rise, with its unseen energy.

I would respond this time, in a non-contemplative way. Arising from my mat, I crawled out and searched for a tall climbable tree with many branches. I found an old Ponderosa pine tree dead many years, with gnarled branches, yet still standing. Its blanched trunk, cast a ghostly pale reflection against the darker trees. Its many branches made climbing easy. Near the top, I surveyed the landscape below. All below me shone as an ocean of forms, in a luminous light spread out under the night sky. It was a sight to behold, as the earth appeared unnatural in this light and augured unnatural responses.

My skin tingled and my hair continued to bristle in excitement, evoking some primal, vestigial, physical response. Little understanding what strange transformation seized me, I was now well along in a process, in which I was a player. No living creature, but I, could respond to the silent call that flooded my rising consciousness. Buried instincts, soul deep and past spent, were reawakening. A lifetime of conditional responses evaporated in this new liberating condition, now free and open.

Not thinking what I was doing there, much less why I was in that tree top, I suddenly felt an urge, a surging NEED TO HOWL. I BEGAN TO BAY AND HOWL AT THE MOON. My head raised up, my jaw dropped, I let up this piercing yell -- long and loud. I howled and howled. The canyon walls took my howls and echoed them on and on, until I again heard the silence, once again close in around me; I bayed again and howled, the sound echoing for miles off the granite cliffs into the absorbing distance. I released so much inner energy, that I experienced a deep contentment and oneness: with all that surrounded me. Fresh new energy entered my body, to replace what I had expelled. I had really started something. *That howling is still echoing out there somewhere* in the universe, somewhere within is vastness, its universal ear is resonating still.

There was a physical price to pay. My sharing the night with the moon, left me physically exhausted and drained the next morning, as though struck down by some force, or power greater than myself. I had been an instrument of something I did not understand.

These encounters led me to write a series of poems, which I titled, "Songs of the High Sierras," celebrating the phenomenon of Nature and its echoes in my spirit. Can the moon really inspire us to howl and sing, write or paint? Well, we know it can move oceans. Why not puny man, that "sack of walking sea water?"

* * * * * * * * *

"Yoga: the control of thought - waves in the mind."

- 200 B.C. Patanjali

9. TRANCE WALKING

It was evening in the Sierra Nevada Mountains. The sun's red glow remained in the western sky, creating a brilliant background for the trees and mountain tops, now shrouded in long growing shadows. It was beautiful to behold; but, I was miles from my camp, with had no light to assist me in returning. My anxiety level was rising as the sun sank out of sight altogether and the after glow slowly disappeared.

Not a good idea to be stumbling around in the dark; yet, here I was, blithely hiking in the fading light. I proceeded walking toward my destination, as the day passed into night. Crossing a long grassy valley, I emerged at the far end, before darkness enveloped me completely. Continuing into a forest stand of tall pines, I relished their fresh scent and felt their presence around me. Feeling reassured, I walked through this forest, my feet finding and keeping to the trail.

As I walked, I heard a roaring mountain stream to my left, and its sound accompanied me on my hike. I wasn't alone after all.

Water, my old friend, was beside me and guiding me. Then, all too soon, my friend left me on my own again and the silence returned.

Could I ever be a friend to the darkness, that now surrounded me? I needed all the help I could get from the dark. I made an invocation from my heart to the night, to protect and guide me on my way. I sensed a kindred spirit, flying overhead. I heard its whirling heavy winds beating the night, I was no more one separate hiker, but moved in concert with a flying guardian guiding each and every footfall.

Huge granite boulders loomed to the right and left, as I then glided between them, their presence more felt than seen. The ground after a time, began to drop off and descend, my feet told me, as I braced my pack, now heavy and tiresome. Yet, still I continued down the side of a mountain, holding to the narrow path in total darkness, feeling in harmony with my guiding spirit.

I felt total confidence in my ability to hike in total darkness. Occasionally a passing star, or several, would appear in the openings overhead. They too, became my companions now, and I noticed their comings and goings with satisfaction. Then I came to a clearing, for I saw the sky open above me, and instantly recognized the Big Dipper on my left. Good, I was still on course, easterly towards Glen Aulin High Sierra Camp.

The clear, dark sky started to affect me subtly at first, then more intensely with each step I took. After a short time I noticed that my backpack's weight was insignificant. This was perplexing to me, for I should have been exhausted after all this hiking, and craving a long rest. Instead, I felt light footed, light hearted, and literally bounded along over rocks and tree stumps, as though I were some airborne bird. With my ultimate goal fixed in my mind, I continued to make remarkable progress. In the darkness, I had no way of seeing where I was stepping, yet unerringly I went my way along. I had to make it to camp -- so nothing would stop me.

If I had stopped to think how impossible all this was, it would have become impossible, and I would have ground to a halt under my own weight. Instead, I was filled with a sense of exhilaration that carried me along. My feet barely grazed the ground, as I effortlessly hiked through the night.

I lost all sense of time, and focused only on the idea of getting to camp, where I could then stop. Then, I saw a camp fire in the distance and knew I had made it. Entering the camp with only the fire to guide me in total darkness, I soon set about putting up my tent. I then quickly crawled in, and went to sleep under a canopy of stars, safe at last.

* * * * * * * * *

On another occasion, while on a hike on Mt. Tamalpias, the reverse occurred. While walking down the mountain, I noticed I was making no progress at all. Time seemed to freeze me in a slow time state, where my feet walked, but gained me little or no ground. I was very disturbed; I felt trapped, unable to continue down the mountain.

While I walked in this state of mind, the objects in the distance remained in the distance, regardless of how much walking I did toward them. I decided to run down the hill in order to break this spell or trance. Nothing changed, and I could make no progress toward even objects a hundred feet ahead of me, regardless of how fast I ran. Is this some cosmic joke on me? Or what?

This is ridiculous, I'm running down a mountain trail, but not getting down at all. It had to be a joke of some kind being played on me by some invisible force. I didn't understand. I was not dreaming, hallucinating or imagining this, I was out walking, when this happened to me -- totally unprepared for what was happening to me. For all my expended energy, I could gain no purchase in movement.

I started to laugh, at my quandary, at my predicament. I saw the illusion of space, clearly, now perhaps of the first time in my life. We don't move in space, but rather we imagine that we move in space. I had been set free from the illusion. I appreciated this insight, and have never forgotten it. We cannot move in space unless we imagine it by creating the illusion: of movement through space.

This was no joke. It was a gift of insight that most will never possibly believe, must less experience. The old philosophical question came to mind, "Why me?" The answer, "why not you?"

Many years later, in reading about Tibet, I discovered that trance-walking is a form of meditation undertaken there, after years of preparation. It is similar to what I had encountered on my night hike. It had somehow occurred to me, without any advance training, or even knowledge of its existence. A new state of being or awareness is tapped by the mind, enabling it to transcend the normal limits of the body, or as in my case, my mind unplugged or disengaged itself from the illusion.

A similar event occurs with runners who get a, "second wind" from their mind, or others who regear their bodies to continue, when they thought they couldn't. Putting one in touch with the surroundings and going with the flow -- we need to learn about how to achieve this state. Too few of us do.

The following story illustrates how all too easy it can be to merge with your surroundings, as you run or walk.

While on a camping trip to the west coast of Baja, California, Mexico, I was walking along a rugged beach of sand dunes, bracing sea breezes, and a pounding surf. The cliff tops were set with wooden shacks of local poor fishermen, who had now finished for the day. All seemed picturesque and still. Waves crashed alongside me, as I walked by the edge of the water. A stiff wind blew in my face off the ocean.

Suddenly, I felt an urge to run. "OK! I'll run," I responded. As I ran or jogged along, I noticed a large seal in the water swimming alongside me. Oh! how gracefully he dives under each wave, only to resurface once again. I caught a glint in his eye and knew at once he was aware of me. More, he was keeping up with me, as I ran along the shore. I'll race him, I thought, and we passed several minutes racing. He bobbed up and down in the water, as I bounded along the sandy edge of the water. Occasionally, I lost sight of him, but then he would resurface and I'd catch that glinting eye again, as he reappeared. He seemed to be pacing me now. I ran for all I was worth and still he outpaced me, always with the small face turning toward me. I could not beat him. Then I realized he had urged me on and sported with me. Oh well, it was an exhilarating race; but, I had no chance against his streamlined body and strong fins. I bade him farewell and started back home, as he disappeared underwater in one last splash.

Silly, yet not so silly, this seal racing. Yes, the big fellow had tricked me and beat me -- I was now sure of it. On reflection, I recalled that I hadn't planned on running that afternoon, as I had run earlier that day. Somehow he influenced me.

The kindredness I felt toward nature and its animal and spirit forces, was leading me toward a break with my body. A parting of the way loomed before me, for which my closeness and oneness with nature had prepared me. I did not know this at the time; yet, I was now to undergo new tests, that would bring me beyond the natural borders, to tap on new doors of the mind and and go beyond it, entering at last into a state of pure consciousness.

These profound changes are always best understood in hindsight; I actually plodded along, into an early encounter with non-physical reality. Lucky for me, I had support for my first tentative steps, into the invisible world beyond our reality.

* * * * * * * * *

PART IV

CHANGES IN MIND/BODY

"It ended...with his body changed to light, a star that burns forever in that sky."

- Aztec

10. WHITE LIGHT

Santa Cruz on the California coast is, as many know, a center for, "new age" exploration. It was with an air of expectancy, that I visited with some friends, at the university there one weekend. The coast line here is rugged and dramatic, cutting through pine forests, as it winds its way towards Big Sur. Sea lions and whales can been seen cavorting offshore. It is as visually exciting and stimulating place, as your likely to find on this planet.

In a small house by the sea, we meet to talk. Then we sat on the floor, that evening, joining hands in a wide circle, in what we hoped would be a spiritual quest. There were seven of us in all, lead by our guide, a spiritual leader.

A certain ambiance was created by the oriental rug on which we sat, the incense burning, the candles glowing, and a general air of shared oneness, in quiet pursuit of something greater than ourselves.

79

This ambiance was necessary to change gears, from our natural state of mental activity, to one of non-activity, and acceptance, and receptivity. Put another way, the thinking process of the brain was turned off, so that the mind was free enough to enter a zone of pure consciousness, unfettered with the concerns and interference normal to its state.

So prepared, we all, joined hands, entering a relaxed state of oneness. Silence reigned, as our leader directed us to concentrate on the energy in the room. This we did and soon sensed its presence. She then instructed us to try and concentrate it into a large ball. This we all set our minds to, and surprise of surprises; we all felt a sense of accomplishment, as *we concentrated the energy into a round ball hovering over our heads.* Next, our leader asked us to try and move this energy ball, around the room in a circle right over our heads. Using our sheer willpower, this large ball began to move, circling over our heads.

We succeeded and our confidence grew at our new found power. She asked us to concentrate on the ball again, and intensify it into a smaller ball. Again, we were able to concentrate it into a smaller ball of great intensity, using sheer willpower and steady concentration.

Now she asked, "Who will receive this energy?" and "Who needs to receive this energy?" My heart leaped up, as I bowed my head in acceptance. *I would receive it,* was instantly communicated to others in the group. All concurred and began to move the now small ball of intense energy, over my head. I prepared myself to receive it, with joy and expectation.

Sitting under it -- *a brilliant white light* slowly dropped down and *entered the top of my head.* I could not see it enter, but felt it enter by its warm glow and heat. I felt very, very good. Bliss replaced fear, while it slowly passed through my head downward into my body. Slowly, it filled me up with its energy, as it entered the void within me.

All at once, I experienced what I can only describe as biological meltdown. Tears flowed down my face, my pores opened with sweat, my heart pounded with utter bliss and fulfillment. *This white heat possessed me* -- became me. I -- it, totally, positively glowed with its all powerful, surfussed energy. I was becoming a human light bulb, a mystic receiving divine enlightenment, like a saint whose lighted halo surrounds him with glowing radiance. I instantly understood the radiance that surrounds sainthood, by direct experience.

Possessed of such unearthly energy, I marveled at its becoming me. Am I so deserving of this divine gift? I have done nothing to deserving this -- I am unworthy, yet I asked to receive it, and it so honored me. It was enough to ask. *It was pure love energy*, for I was filled with contentment, all I could handle and then some -- I was overflowing with it.

Sitting with my arms resting on my legs, my hands curled upwards, allowing the light to curve back into me, as it made a circuit through my body, back to my head in an unbroken circle, and concentrating its effect on me -- holding it within me. Time seemed to stand still, I had no thought, no conceptions beyond utter fulfillment. I HAD ENTERED A STATE OF PURE BEING AND BECAME A RADIANT BEING.

My friends were gazing at me in astonishment, at this seeming miracle, they were witnessing. Then, the light slowly reemerged out of the top of my head and seemed to diffuse throughout the room once again. I collapsed on the rug and my friends attempted to raise me up. I was drained by the experience; and only after sipping some herbal tea, was I myself again.

Afterwards, we shared our perceptions of what had occurred. All agreed that the light entered my head, and suffused me in a glowing radiance, only to depart minutes later out of my head. All agreed that it was a positive or *spiritual force*. It also had a healing effect, as it dispelled all sense of wrongness, in all of us. I felt more wholeness than at any time of my life and that I was forever changed.

We parted, perhaps never to see this white light again, yet its memory is strong and burns still in my mind. When will it again enter my body?, that is always a question for me. Is it the most powerful healing force that exists? I am sure, it is just that. What was this force? Have there been documented events of its power before?

Yes, throughout history. For years later, I read of similar experiences. The white light was called *cosmic power*. It is not easily obtained, but is accessible to those who seek it and possess a pure heart.

While this awakening to cosmic power, occurred with friends, in a controlled environment, I was totally unprepared for what was to follow...and to follow and follow.

* * * * * * * * *

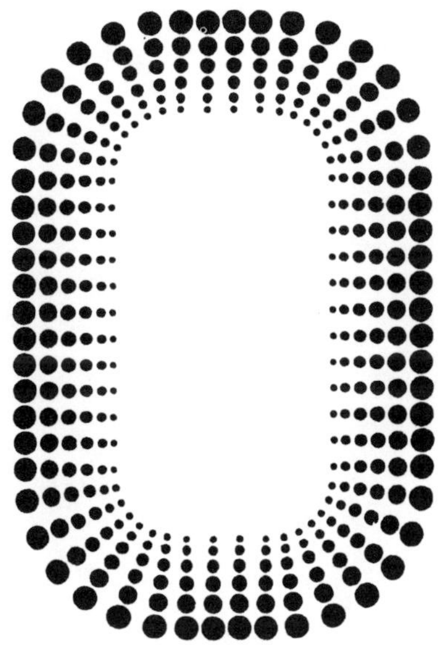

" As in a mirror,so it is seen
  here in the Self."

        Katha Upanishad

11. O.B.E. I

Cold winds banked the clouds atop the Rocky Mountains. Evening light faded into darkness, as we started driving out of Vail, Colorado, west toward Utah. The slopes of Vail are a favorite haunt of mine, so it was with mixed feelings that I started homeward.

The snow drifts along the mountain road began to give way to tufts of grass and brush, as we descended out of the high passes and onto the plains of Utah. Then it happened.

As the car made its final descent out onto the plain, along a long incline, the car lights died. We were suddenly plunged into total darkness. We were traveling at about 65 miles per hour on icy roads, which meant breaking would make the car spin out of control. There was nothing left, but to hold it steady and gradually slow down to a stop, as quickly as possible. The only problem with this was that I couldn't see the road -- it was blind driving. I tried to visualize the roadway, as I started down the long incline where it entered the plain below.

God help us, I prayed, as I grit my teeth. My girlfriend slept soundly, oblivious to it all in the back seat. The car must have blown the light fuse -- boy what timing. Yet, it could have blown sooner, on the passes, where our chances would have been nil.

I realized things could be even worse. The car appeared to be doing well. I felt it level off on the ground as we entered the plain. So far, so good. I continued to depress the brakes, while holding the car on course, and slowed it gradually to 55, then 45, then...

The car left the road and began shaking violently up and down in the sandy, rutted ground, as it pitched headlong into a deep ditch. My heart sank with despair and fear. Shock as...

I WATCHED THE CAR FALL INTO THE DITCH, down some six feet or so, until only its rear end was visible in the distance, where it had finally came to a complete stop.

What a close call that was, I thought, from my vantage point, not realizing that I was now several hundred yards up the mountain road, among rocks and trees, watching the car on the plains below.

My vantage point kept me a safe distance from the crash. Then it slowly dawned on me, that I was not in the car. I was not in my body. Where was I? Fear flooded my senses and my heart froze with the incredible realization that, *I was where I couldn't be, outside my body.* Why? How? What...? I had really left my body, probably to escape bodily harm. I had succeeded, or had I? In my panic, I had involuntarily left my body in the car, where it still must be somehow. I observed the car through the darkness. It was upright and had not overturned. Good, I thought. Somehow I felt reassured, yet was mentally upset and fearful. Was I dead -- the ultimate escape? I had better find out -- I floated down somehow to the car below, to see if my body was OK. I was very scared. Inside the car, the body, mine, didn't seem damaged at all. The next thing I knew, I was slumped over the wheel like a tossed doll - but ok physically. I knew I was back in my body again -- how I reentered, I still don't know, because it took no time or thought about doing it. It just happened -- easier than putting on my jacket, which takes some time.

I heard my girlfriend asking, "What happened?" I explained how we went off the road. I then checked myself out. Just soreness in all my joints and a numbness, more induced by fear than pain.

I was somewhat disorientated as well and unbelieving of where I was. But otherwise, physically in good shape -- then a sense of relief swept through me, and a sense of letting the fear go. I could stay in my body -- it was OK -- flashed through my mind a final time. The numbness remained with me however.

We climbed out of the car, slowly opening the front and rear doors, and climbed out of the ditch. The car's wheels were stuck in the sand. It would have to be towed.

The stars shown brightly, in a moonless desert sky overhead, as we walked back to the road. After 10 or 15 minutes, a huge truck came down the road toward us. We waved and shouted until it stopped before us. We told the driver of our accident. He kindly drove us into the next town.

After a night in a motel, we accompanied a tow truck back to get our car. After towing it back to town and having it checked out, we discovered that the light fuse had blown, and the wheel alignment was a mess.

"You know it could have been a lot worse for you youngsters," the old repairman stated. "How right you are," I replied, recalling those sharp turns on the mountain passes. Visions of twisted metal at the bottom of the canyon flashed before my eyes.

After lunch, we were back on the road and I told my girlfriend, with some guilt, how I had left my body, before the car hit the ditch. We concluded it was an, "out of body experience."

I recalled the story another friend had told me, of a similar experience years before.

* * * * * * * * *

She and her dog were walking along a trail, when all of a sudden she was in the sky. She did not realize this at first, as she observed herself and her dog, Butch, walking below. "That's me and Butch walking down there," she said to herself, until she finally realized she was also in the sky, and out of her body.

In her case it was a spontaneous experience with no fear involved. My experience was fear-driven, but no less real. It was intense and stressful and had left me numb with fear.

This uncanny ability to leave our bodies is difficult to explain. Some claim to be able to induce it themselves, although my experience has been that it was spontaneous, or induced by extreme stress. It is an experience that occurs commonly enough to be believable by many today: it is called O.B.E. (Out of Body Experience).

Can our spirit, or mind, or consciousness change or alter once it has left our body? I believe that it can and does, but that it is another story.

My own conclusion is that my mind (or spirit), separated from my body with extreme ease and seemed receptive to alteration in this state of separation.

What is so amazing, is the ease with which it is possible to separate off from our bodies. Our mind or consciousness is really not bound, permanently to our body. Our body appears to be a temporary place of abode for it (and a risky place to dwell in). I am now convinced that when our body is no longer functional, our mind (spirit) permanently checks out of it, into its ongoing state of eternal consciousness. Those left behind refer to this event as, "Passing On." Another word for it is death, the "D" word. This is a hard word for people to say, much less accept. We embrace the temporal body and fear our eternal state, which is in reality, our true state, which is ongoing and permanent.

Seen in this light the O.B.E. (Out of Body Experience) is a rehearsal for death, a preview if you will, of what will come to us all eventually. Seen another way, it is our re-entry into the invisible world of pure energy that pervades all things. I believe that we can re-enter once again into the material world of visible forms, a temporal phase, if our consciousness wills it. However, at this point I don't know the ground rules.

A different experience altogether awaited me in Northern Italy, which was unbelievable, since I have never heard of anyone who has experienced it, either before or since. I have never met anyone who believes me -- but it happened!

* * * * * * * * *

"If the doors of perception were cleansed everything would appear to man as it is, infinite."

- W. Blake

12. O.B.E. II

Facing the central square of Florence, Italy, stands an imposing building known as the Uffizi Museum. Built of handhewn rock during the Renaissance, it houses some of the finest art of its period.

As I was walking through its hallways, I attempted to avoid a large tour group, by ducking into a room off to one side of the passageway. Here I was alone in a small room, filled with early Renaissance religious paintings. I was the only person in the room, so I was able to view the painting totally undisturbed. Paintings of saints and sinners hung all around me. I noted St. Jerome in the wilderness, surrounded by animals. His cardinal hat lay tossed on the ground. His eyes were filled with spiritual intensity as looked within.

My eye was then attracted to a painting of the Annunciation, by Simone Martini. This subject was a favorite of the early masters, as it portrays the interaction of the divine and the human world. These attempts to capture moments of religious intensity fascinated me. Years of studying Art History had made me familiar with the artists' fervor and devotion.

This particular painting struck me differently. Divine light streamed down from the heavens and illuminated the face of the Blessed Virgin Mary. She is portrayed as an innocent, receiving this unearthly light. In addition, there are halos of divine light, surrounding the heads of the angel and Mary herself. I concentrated on the light streaming into the figures and around their heads.

I saw the words of the angel stream into Mary...It was with a slow dawning realization that I discovered, *I was no longer looking at the painting, but had entered it.* Somehow, I had been pulled into the hanging painting of the Annunciation and was for lack of better words possessed by it, displaced by it somehow.

My body remained outside this new found existence (being inside a work of art). It was a new world where, *my body could not enter.* The feeling was one of *curiosity and eeriness* at being displaced outside myself. I was not at all frightened at my new state of being -- I accepted it freely, with gratitude. I existed (somehow) in this uneasy state. The sensation was new to me and disturbing on another level. I felt like I was in a strange force field, of some kind, unable to escape or even move -- I was frozen into it.

Just being there, was all I was capable of doing. I had become the painting itself, as unbelievable as this sounds. Time stopped; indeed, my life stopped. I hung on the wall as art.

Light streamed down upon me and suddenly my uneasiness departed. The light inside, and around me, *held me in a positive way;* so that *I felt good and happy.* The feelings of these moments were entirely subjective. The feeling of energy and warm nurturing light embraced me lovingly. My spirits continued to rise, uplifted by this glory of finding myself, in this new state of being. I was changed into a *new being of light.*

I entered a state of blissful fulfillment in this painting, forgetting everything, but the presence of the divine light that suffused my entire consciousness. I was at one with everything and at peace. I myself counted for nothing, as I formerly had known myself, as a separate being. Just as suddenly, as I had entered the painting, I left it. (Art was no more -- me I was).

I was once again observing the angel and Mary, from outside the painting. I was back in my body, as easily as I had left it. Now, I was frightened at what happened to me. I stepped back from the painting to observe its frame and the wall on which it hung. I had to convince myself that I was now outside the painting again. I looked around the room at the other paintings. St. Jerome across the room continued to look within.

I wondered if I had had a mystic experience. I had never heard of this happening to anyone I knew of. I had never even read about such an occurrence. Yet, I did lose all control over myself and *entered the painting*, of this I had no doubt. But people can't disappear into paintings or works of art. "Or can they?", I asked myself. I had been taken into it without my thinking about it. I was totally unprepared for what had happened to me: a brief existence as an oil painting, it was absurd.

More, it had a frightening aspect to it, as I did not will this to happen. I was not in control; but, now I felt relieved to be out again. But the painting was no longer alive; its full force had retreated back into itself. Its energy was gone, the room seemed empty again. I stood in awe and amazement at what had happened to me. While frightening, it was glorious and blissful. Would I ever experience this again? It was after all a glorious state of being, for inside the painting, I had become a being of light, a new state of being that I did not know existed.

My mind began to question itself. Did I imagine all this? The absurdity of the question caused me to smile. I knew that I could not imagine bliss and glory, or feel it overwhelm me. No, this was beyond imagination. And my mind boggled, as it appeared that something had possessed me. I had no doubt now of this complete change in my consciousness; to become a non-man - - a being of pure, divine light.

Again my mind sought alternatives. Was it a vision? The act of seeing things invisible? I knew it was a state of being, that I had never encountered before. Had others? The visions of St.

Jerome in the wilderness; how real were they? Beating his chest with a rock, seeking a vision of God. He, too, saw the Divine light and pursued his vision of the divine state of being. His rejection of the religious life -- throwing away his cardinal hat -- was proof of that.

Can we open our eyes and see, beyond seeing? We must leave our eyes behind to see the invisible. Indeed, we must leave our bodies and our brain behind, to really perceive the invisible.

I believe many saints did achieve glimpses, visions of this invisible world, most of us today deny in our ignorance.

* * * * * * * * *

13. PREFIGURATION

The old train creaked and swayed as it rolled into the main rail terminal of Rome. My eyes started to tear -- cry almost, without my knowing why. Sitting in my compartment, I was somewhat embarrassed as it was full of travelers. "Is this your first visit to Rome?" a Swedish woman asked me. Answering in the affirmative, I sense this was not altogether true.

Why were these confounding tears flowing -- what is it with me? As I groped for answers -- I had a mysterious feeling of having been in this city before, yet I knew that it couldn't be.

After finding a congenial hostel in the city, I ventured out to the Palatine Hill, which overlooks the Forum. This is the heart of the Ancient City, sprawling ruins of crumbling walls and monuments, arches and marble statuary.

The Palatine is now a very peaceful hillside, covered with grass and wildflowers. Here and there, one can still see the remains of foundations and stones piled on stones, that are now almost covered with weeds and flowers. Old palaces and villas, now all but disappeared, are being reclaimed by the earth. A certain picturesque obscurity reigned over this hillside, now gone silent in the heat of this summer day.

As I mused on this tranquil scene, the pealing of a bell rang out. Looking for its source, I noticed an old Franciscan Monastery with stone walls and a bell tower, all well-preserved, that sat in a small valley below me.

A line of brown-robed monks moved toward an archway, passing into the monastery to observe vespers. In the charm of this idyllic scene, I saw a direct link to its past. It was like seeing into its past, past the ruins around me. All appeared to be a prefiguration, of what I knew not, except its compelling call to me.

I continued to explore the precincts around the hill. Soon I came upon some tall free-standing walls of crumbling brick. Then I wandered into a large enclosure. As I walked, I gazed up at the weed-covered walls to discover, I was inside the Ancient Baths of Caraculla.

Fragments and patches of very old mosaics and tiles could still be seen on the walls in some chambers. All was on a grand scale. The huge chambers were silent and in state of decay; yet, life abounded here at one time.

Eternal silence enveloped me. I was enraptured with a keen sense of time past -- all pointed to the past. Totally relaxed, a wave of contentment overtook me -- like being at home. Eternal silence.

Until, I heard a startling sound. What? Well -- it was water! Yes, I could now clearly hear water, WATER, splashing water in this dry, crumpled ruin. Did my ears deceive me? I knew there was no water here -- unless there was an old fountain, still running into some deep pool of standing water.

I encountered no water as I searched, yet the sound grew louder and louder, then laughter and people talking, lots of people. *All around me sounds echoed off the walls*, of crowds of *active people*, milling about laughing and talking. The *water sounds* of splashing and bubbling continued, as if I were in a crowded bath. Occasionally, I made out the sound of wet cloth towels slapping against the stones (washing?). Women were talking loudly between themselves as they washed clothes.

Still, I saw nothing, only my ears heard the tumultuous din, the sounds of happy people. Was I imagining this, or had I inadvertently crossed into their space time? Was I there, or were they here? The space here was alive with sounds of activity, and yet it could not be so, I knew. There was no one here -- no people, no water, only silence and me. My brain resisted..."You must be imagining all this," it accused me relentlessly. My mind retorted, "you are not perceiving reality." My consciousness flowed on in spite of both.

A rising sense of exhilaration overcame my arguments with myself, my reserve, and I let myself go to be there with them. It was a charged atmosphere of life and smells and sounds. A crowded huge chamber teemed with sounds of unintelligible language. The laughs and the cries were clearly discernible against the general din.

Then, I smelled flowers all around me, but couldn't see them. Still, I was within it, of it, yet could see nothing. Captivated, I reveled in this revelry, and delighted in this psychic glimpse of the past. Still I wasn't up to seeing it; this sense had failed me. But, I was one with it, felt it, heard it, smelled and sensed it -- the cool walls, the water...joy in its revelry held me transfixed. Nothing distracted me from the encounter. I let go of all doubts. I no longer questioned it. My mind plunged into the encounter, head-long and unafraid. For this I was thankful, the letting go, the openness of it, the willingness, the trust of it was complete! Letting go of reason, of logic...of the mind itself.

I was being there in the past with them again.

A bitter-sweet feeling of sadness and happiness hung like a pall over me until...caught in the vines of time...Misty vales obscured solidity -- sensation only of being, pure being, until...I noticed a fern growing atop that wall and the silence had returned. Yes, it was over...whatever it had been. My brain reassured command over my senses; or, so it would have me believe. A deep sadness at its disappearance (the experience) overcame me.

Eternal silence reigned once more. My mind (spirit) had returned (the past was dead here). Emotional contact too, was now broken - the questioning mind resumed its duties: present time was reestablished.

How long this experience lasted, I haven't a clue. (Does it matter?) I walked onto the hill again -- a sea of wildflowers lay before me. I started down the hill toward the Forum, on a long and overgrown grassy path, back to the center of the eternal city.

Did I return to the past? This question flooded my mind all that day. It is one of those questions of which there is no definitive answer. I was, however, thankful for the experience, which was a vivid and vital glimpse of a past world. I could only sense, and then just briefly, if at all, a visit to the past, which is, we are told, no more.

* * * * * * * * *

<pre>
"Our birth is but a sleep
 and a forgetting."
</pre>

Wordsworth

14. STRANGE ENCOUNTERS

Following are a series of episodic events that remain in the realm of the unexplained:

As a boy of fifteen or so, I was out alone one night walking home. It was a clear starry night, summer I recall. I also remember the scent of freshly-cut grass hanging in the warm air.

I became aware of something different, something new, I expected something to happen. As I looked up in to the sky, I saw a large object crossing overhead. I stopped in my tracks, amazed at its hugeness. In shape, it was like a fat cigar -- very long -- hundreds of feet at least. Along its side, I clearly could see a row of round windows. The object was moving slowly. My immediate reaction was -- what is that? It was strangely quiet, as though it were watching me. I felt violated at being observed by this thing that shouldn't be there in the sky. It was vastly larger than any airplane and it was too long to be a dirigible.

107

It had windows along its entire length. It then passed out of my view, leaving all the night sky empty, save for the stars. I often wondered about this childhood sighting and what it was. I have never seen another one like it.

Many years later, I have come to believe, and belief is as strong as I can make it -- there are no proofs -- that anyone who sights or experiences a U.F.O. (Unidentified Flying Objects) is forever changed, and will thereafter see things differently. You cannot help but be changed, when something unknown touches you. It is a violation of all you have been taught to believe: it remains outside explainable reality. All we can do at this time is ask questions, founded on our physical understanding of reality, which is incomplete, as it does not address the energy level of reality, which is after all -- most of it.

The U.S. government has acknowledged U.F.O.'s exist.

Years later, I heard of a pilot for a commercial airliner, whose description of a flying cigar with windows, matched my own childhood observation. Like me, he was unsure of what he saw, and asked the stewardess if anyone on the flight were awake and had seen anything. The stewardess found one male passenger, who was awake, and invited him forward to talk to the pilot. This passenger had also seen this flying object, but with something more, a shape looking out of one of the round windows, along its cigar length.

The pilot has recounted that in all his twenty - five years of flying, he has encountered only this one sighting; one he could not explain by any known means. To this day, numerous sightings continue to be reported -- all unexplained. I believe they are not from outer space, but from other dimensions, which materialize here on their appointed rounds.

Sitting in a graduate seminar on the structure of Shakespeare's <u>Anthony and Cleopatra</u>, I was somewhat uneasy with the seemingly petty turn the discussion had taken. The detail was obscuring the message of this great tragedy. We were missing a wonderful opportunity. It's important to understand the structure of Shakespeare's language; but my mind left the room and entered the play itself, out of boredom at our not getting the message of this play. I experienced no control over this leave-taking. It was spontaneous, immediate and involuntary.

The message was more important than the language, and my mind took off in search of it. I was instantly transported to the world of Egypt, and saw a living Anthony and Cleopatra before me. I was immediately seized by the realization of their great love for each other -- it was a transcending love that overshadowed any petty tragedies occurring to them. Language itself was inadequate to convey their world; it still existed, as I witnessed it numerous centuries later. I was OBSERVING their love firsthand, not merely reading about it, speculating about it, or imagining it. Their living presence before me was no apparition. I actually felt their presence, their love, and its consuming power.

The most unbelievable thing of all, was their *love, pure energy that existed still,* in a form that you could feel and visit like the eternal pyramids -- it was a living monument of love -- still! The clashing armies have vanished, yet their love lived on, in this state. The words merely point the way; it is for mind to discover, to leap beyond, to discover hidden mines of pure being, that still exist in dimensions beyond our own.

Coming back, my mind picked up the discussion of a lead-in phrase to an object word. I smiled at the professor, in acknowledgement at this point of information. Yes, no doubt about it, the word was him, the object. The nominal holds sway over the phenomenal: the word over the experience. My experience was admirably transcendental and similar in some respects to my Art O.B.E.

* * * * * * * * *

Disease lies alongside the margins of life; fighting off a flu virus is never easy. It is a long process, often days and weeks, even years, until it is vanquished, or it maims and kills.

Our conception of the virus itself is usually an abstract one, as it must be seen under a microscope, magnified hundreds of times. Even then, all one can see are tiny, squiggly lines or dots. In the dream state, our mind sometimes is able to visualize disease in a way our waking mind cannot. I discovered this while fighting off the flu myself. During a dream, I was able to visualize the virus as it attacked my system.

The first visualization was of a series of protuberances emerging out of an internal landscape of parts of my body. They were ugly and twisted, bulging eruptions in the membranes of my body, an internal war zone, showing the effects the virus had wrought on me. How accurate these visualizations are, can only be the stuff of speculation at this point in our evolution. We need to learn more about how to do this.

The second visualization was of a death image of a man, strangely pockmarked, who stared gloomily at me: a look that was angry and threatening. I sought to block out this image and not think about it, upon waking. The visualization seemed more of the typical image in this genre. The extent to which we can influence change in our body, through visualization, is a hopeful sign in our evolution.

On another occasion while hitchhiking into San Francisco one day, I got a ride from a man who exuded the feeling of death. There were no visible clues whatsoever to sustain my belief that he represented death, to anyone who came into contact with him. My immediate aim was to escape his threatening presence. As the car stopped for a red light, I quickly exited the car saying, "I changed my mind," about going to San Francisco with him. I relied solely on what I can only describe as *vibrations, emanations,* and *feelings* about him. I had however, learned long ago, to trust these sensations.

A few months later, in talking to a friend, I learned she had also accepted a ride, along with a girlfriend of hers, from him. They too, sensed something wrong about him, and asked to get out before going too far. He stopped the car and let them out saying they were, "very lucky," to escape him. He had planned to "kill you both," he freely admitted, if they had stayed. They walked into town, scared out of their wits, yet relieved to be alive. Their description of him fit every detail of my own recollection of him.

Some inner intelligence awaits all of us, if we would listen to it, and heed it. Often, there are no visible clues, no facts to help us decide what to do, or how to do it. It could even be a form of animal instinct still untapped by most people. Yet, we must trust this *inner voice* to guide us, because it knows everything, somehow, on a deeper conscious level, that is accessible to us, if we would but listen to it. Some call it intuition.

The following episode from my youth is one that is, to this day, embarrassing to me. It is one I wish never occurred -- a childhood case of spite and ill-will and for which I plead guilty and ask forgiveness.

I was about sixteen years old and on a trip to Canada with my Aunt Katherine and my mother, brother and sister. We had been driving north through New England, on our way to Quebec, to visit the shrine of St. Anne. This was a pilgrimage that our family always enjoyed traveling to, and except for the long prayers we were asked to repeat by Aunt Katherine along the way, the trips were a high point of our lives.

We decided to stop overnight in a rural inn in northern Vermont. After booking in, we raced up the stairs to find our respective rooms in this old Victorian mansion. I found a room I loved, and set about unpacking, when Aunt Katherine entered and told me to leave, as this was "her room." Choking on my deep disappointment, I looked her in the eye and told her, "someone died in that bed." She ushered me out and claimed the bed as her own. I was forced to bunk with my brother that night.

The following morning at breakfast, she upbraided me with, "I couldn't sleep all night," as evidently what I said had so unsettled her that she, "could get no rest that night." I quickly told her that I was, "very sorry," and had made it up in anger. She never forgave me, all the same, to her dying day.

Like ideas, our words and emotions have consequences beyond our knowledge. We bear a special responsibility for them, just as we do for our acts.

* * * * * * * * *

"Half our days we pass in the shadow of the Earth: and the brother of Death exacteth a third part of our lives."

- Sir Thomas Browne

15. UNKNOWN MORPHOLOGIES

A bird threw itself at the window again and again; its body hit the glass with surprising force. The vibrations were almost enough to shatter the glass. Sitting by the fireplace, my wife asked loudly, "What is it doing that for?" Trying to find some rational answer, I offered, "Maybe it is disorientated or sick," in a quiet reassuring way. Yet, I remained disturbed by this unsettling assault on my home. It was too bizarre.

Walking over to the window, I saw it strike the glass, yet again, as it made eye contact with me. Then it flew off and disappeared into the trees. An eerie sense of unnaturalness overwhelmed me. How strange, how odd, I thought. What could it mean? I had no answers. Deep within me the questions resounded, and a growing coldness enveloped my consciousness.

Within an hour, a deep realization overwhelmed me; Aunt Katherine had died. Yes, she was dead, I thought. I was not absolutely sure of it, so I did nothing. Later that same evening, the telephone rang. My wife answered it, and I knew it was my mother now calling, to confirm my worst fears. She then told me of Katherine's passing that evening. A sinking depression hit me, as I recalled long childhood summers spent with Aunt Katherine and Grandmother. Now, they were both dead. A void opened up within me, that I could never fill.

Years later, I discussed this event with my mother. She agreed with me, believing that it was possible to transmit messages using paranormal methods. She told me stories of her childhood and of recently dead Irish relations, visiting close ones on their way to the "Next Life." Indeed, every Irish family knows of such occurrences, particularly in the old country. She said if it were all possible, she herself would attempt to, "visit me and make herself known to me." I agreed to watch for her, after she passed on to the next life. She nodded. She had always maintained a deep and abiding interest in things unknown, the occult and paranormal side of life.

Many years afterward, I lay in bed one morning in a deep sleep, when the phone began to ring. It was about six-thirty A.M. Half awake, I realized my mother had died unexpectedly during the night. I burrowed under the covers to blot out this premonition.

I told myself there was no way she could have died, that I had talked to her a few days ago, and would visit her in Florida the next weekend. She wouldn't die, if I was coming to visit her, I thought.

Shortly afterward the phone started to ring again. It was seven A.M. Again, I refused to answer and acknowledge this horrible and totally unacceptable event. After persistent ringing, it finally stopped. I was safe -- it didn't happen.

I dozed off in reassurance once again.

At seven-thirty, the phone rang again. It would keep ringing until I answered it, I reasoned. Picking up the receiver, I heard my brother's sad voice confirming my worst fears. She had passed away in the middle of the night, and he had waited until morning to call me.

Then I recalled a final meeting with my parents outside their home in Florida. As I was getting into my car to leave them, *I felt it was the last time I would see them together alive.* Hesitating, I wanted to go over and hug them both, but this was never done in our family. My mother sensing my delay said, "I think you better get going, Billy." As I pulled out of the driveway, I watched them wave goodbye. Their aged, shrunken figures etched in my mind. It was their final joint farewell; and now my mother too, had passed on.

Several months passed, when one morning I was startled out of my sleep, by a rabbit-sized animal crawling across my bed, In the pre-dawn light, it appeared furry and barely visible in the dim light. It then circled my bed in an exploratory curious way, which bewildered and frightened me. As I watched it, it watched me, then it disappeared. There were no wall openings or window openings out of which it could pass, but pass it did, out of the room. It was bizarre and unnatural behavior for an animal. I sensed something, non-worldly had happened -- something that frightened me very much.

This could be no ordinary animal. This had been mother paying me a visit, as she promised. Yet, I could not verify it. Since she visited me, I would return the visit, for she had, I thought, fulfilled her promise to contact me some way, somehow. I asked her, deep within myself, for further proof from the "other side," as she so often phrased it. I was to wait a long time for my reply and forgot the question before it was answered years later.

As soon as I got the chance, I made a trip to visit her grave site in Connecticut. I was accompanied by a young woman friend, who I had known for years. As we made our visit, and were enjoying the fall foliage in the cemetery, we decided to sit on the grass covering her grave.

It was like a picnic but without the food. The scents of decaying leaves filled the air in a preternatural way, that I somehow expected. I observed the yew tree mother had ordered me to cut back away from her grave stone, a tall Vermont marble. Yes, all was as she would have wanted it. I had also forgotten my request, for a second proof from her.

Sitting there in a calm way felt good, and I sensed a closeness to mother. Then I noticed, my young friends's *face gradually began to change.* I blinked my eyes to stare at her face, only to see *an older face emerging -- that of my mother's --* only her face was changed, to that of my mother's, not her body. It was so uncanny and paralyzing, I was numb with amazement. She looked with soulful eyes right through me, and I thanked her for this final proof, from beyond, just as she had promised, from beyond the grave. I nodded my head. It was scary and reassuring at the same moment.

Still, I was very frightened by this manifestation and could barely remain calm. Once I acknowledged her presence, *her face slowly changed back very slowly*, gradually to my friend's face, who emerged with an open innocent look of acceptance, yet unaware anything had occurred to her.

I blinked at her in a heightened state of agitation, for I was unnerved by what had happened; and we hastily left the cemetery. I told my friend nothing of this experience, not wanting to agitate her, as I knew it could. Now, I had two personal encounters with mother and was grateful for her willingness to reach out to me, as she had promised.

I had not counted on how frightened they would leave me -- these returns.

In order to handle this experience, I put in out of my mind, at least for the time being until I began my journal, where it is recounted in print for the first time. It had been too frightening to face before writing about it. Perhaps the printed word lends it a safe remove from reality and I am better able to handle it this way.

By "rational" standards, this will seem an overactive imagination or worse. It is and remains unprovable; yet I know that what happened to me has happened to others, and will continue to happen in the future. Such occurrences are recognized by people of all cultures. Additional close calls with death have been frequent.

There is an old Maidu Indian saying, "A tree could kill you, if it wanted to." I was hit by a tree falling on top of my head and was knocked down, but merely bloodied. On another occasion, a tree fell on my house destroying my roof, but spared me. I sleep but six feet from its final resting spot. I now consider that trees don't wish to kill me, but wish me to know that they can, a communication I have long acknowledged.

Death is no longer a revelation in modern science. It has become a formality, a ritual. Among the Austrailian Aboriginal, family members often sense the death, or coming death, of a family member. The vision of a rooster is seen as a precursor of death, followed by a sinking depression of spirit -- until the cause is discovered -- death of a close loved one. Then certain tribal members assist the family with active participation and ceremony, for a life hereafter. These certain members must be of moieties that harbor death. Other moieties harbor life and their tasks are life orientated ones.

In Irish tradition, the bird getting into the cottage, was a harbinger of a death in the family. One cued to omens could often read these as signs -- predicting oncoming events. It implied an extra sensitivity to things beyond normal understanding. In Ireland, the "Fey," members of each clan, possessed precognition and recognition beyond the visible world. Sadly, the modern Irish are losing these special, age-old abilities and their recognition of wonderful moieties.

In our modern age, we now refer to E.S.P. (Extra Sensory Perception) as the 5th Dimension, for it evokes a hidden, older grasp of our abilities to know things and it is the key to opening the doors to the invisible world. Notwithstanding, death is part of this world, and a state not to be feared.

Incidently, animals possess E.S.P. as do plants -- to what extent must remain the stuff of speculation.

I must now pass along to the hidden realms of the cosmic world where all things are possible, but will recount only my personal experience in these realms and my beliefs about them.

* * * * * * * * *

PART V

BEYOND THE LIMITS

"The universe and our world is a place of inexhaustable, unseen forms..."

Kazimir Malevich, Russian Painter

16. COSMIC ENERGY

Throughout this book, I refer to forces, spirits, white light, etc.; but I have not gone into my views of what I believe is the nature of this energy field, what constitutes this field and creates this invisible world. This was intentional, as I wished to dwell on my personal interaction with these forces. In this chapter, I will depart from my journal format and attempt to backup and describe this force, insofar as words describe it.

It is not mere energy or physical reality as we know it. Scientists do not study it, nor do most of them acknowledge its existence in the universe, preferring instead to study its effects on the physical plane under a number of terms, that shift like shadows of clouds across a lake.

It is multi-dimensional and outside time and space limitations, which makes it impossible to study using our tools -- words and measures limited to three dimensions. Incidently, why aren't U.F.O.'s under serious study? For these same reasons?

Anyone who has experienced this cosmic energy will agree, that it is best described simply as LOVE. Cosmic energy is ultimately LOVE, the drink, the food we eat, the trees and ground we stand on, the stars in the sky, our very bodies are such stuff as love, the molecules that blissfully compose our universe -- all are love generated. Love is life; death and change are love.

Now this sounds naively simple, until - you have achieved or experienced Realization. It is a reality beyond proofs. It is a Metaphysical Reality, a non-physical reality. It is a greater reality than our own, as it fills the spaces between our hollow atoms and holds it altogether, like some etheric glue. This holistic view of reality is the ultimate one and, mystery of mysteries, it is one, inseparable whole, ever-changing without beginning or end -- eternal and godlike. If I am correct in this belief, why do so few experience this realization, this bliss? Sadly, it is too mystical, or holistic for many to accept, much less understand, or even accept as a remote possibility. They prefer the passive shadows, the explanations of science, the media-truth which perpetuates the lie that love is really sex dressed up and civilized, or that love is romance, idealized in a thousand ways to titillate the public.

Witness the media event of the 1960's. The headlines across America, indeed the world, declared it, the "Love Generation."

Tabloids pictured "Sex Crazed Hippies," and "Free Love." These media labels defined and isolated a whole generation of youth who, unlike their parents, opened their hearts and minds to love and its power to change their world. The media hype worked and a consciousness-raising movement was stereotyped and made a thing of ridicule. Notwithstanding, the realization of the universal nature of love persisted. God is love we can say and we are all of him, representing aspects of Him. He is not some deity in the sky watching us, living in some unworldly paradise. We are Him and He is us -- *we need but look within to find Him.*

On a human level, I believe that this Cosmic Energy, this Love, is generated throughout the universe (we are never cut off from it), as a force field that manifests in feelings, emotions, and vibrations felt by all of us. In short, it is more in evidence in some than in others -- still others seem starved of it. Yet, love is there for all of us; we are literally creatures of love and, if we recognize this, we would recognize it in others, including animals, plants and all natural objects.

My tapping into this Cosmic Energy, this Love, has made this abundantly clear to me on many levels. Anyone who has experienced a transcendental event, knows that love lies at the heart of it. Making contact with this realization brings bliss.

What authorities can do! Starting with the family, school, society, media, scientists, the government, and organized religion, we have layer upon layer of hardening-of-the-arteries in human consciousness. What is over looked by so many is that love generation is something altogether new. It is a new consciousness of our human nature, a new awareness of love itself, as something transcending all borders and limits placed upon it: a force greater than ourselves.

This, ultimately, is what love generation is. We need to tap its cosmic applications in our lives and fundamental beings. LOVE IS THE ESSENTIAL FORCE IN CREATION, its building blocks and the mortar of our vast universe, the all pervasive energy that holds it altogether -- COSMIC ENERGY.

Our consciousness is the key to opening ourselves to receiving this force, this COSMIC ENERGY. Whatever cuts us off from this force denies something fundamental to our evolution.

* * * * * * * * *

*"We are such stuff as dreams are made of, and our little life
is rounded with a sleep."*

- Shakespeare

17. VISION QUEST

The North American Indians had a mystical ceremony that
is little known to us today. It consisted of the male members of the
tribe going out in to the wilderness (while women and children
offered sacrifices for them) in their quest for a vision. This vision
was a gift to the tribe and all shared in it. The male Indian would
wander alone in the forest, or mountains often naked, with little
food, to seek help from the "Great Spirit," to show the way
through life and beyond death. If the Indian succeeded, in having
a vision and more often than not, he did not succeed, he could
share it with the whole tribe on his return.

A wild celebration then took place, to honor the helpful
spirits that guided the Indian people, as well as the departed ones,
for whom a general lamentation was set up. Dancing was another
means of achieving a vision, as the spirit left the body during its
frenzied movements.

On a vision quest of my own, I set off with friends into
California's mighty mountains once again. We headed toward the

back country, where only backpackers can go. We set up camp near a roaring waterfall with a stream at its base, flowing into a small valley deep in the Sierra Nevadas. The next day, we climbed up to some rocky cliffs where deep alpine lakes with crystal pure, blue waters reflected the white clouds passing rapidly overhead. We came onto a meadow. The grass was dotted with wildflowers -- Paint Brush, Lupines and Black-eyed Susans. A gentle wind was blowing and each flower seemed to bow its head in seemingly welcome, as we crossed the meadow.

We retired after sunset and woke the next morning, caught some golden trout and cooked them in wild sage -- what a treat, I thought. Later that very morning, I went off on my vision quest.

A day passed alone, then on the second day the isolation seemed to weigh on me, until I went climbing up atop some loose boulders. The sun began to rise in the eastern sky. I sat down after a tough climb to catch my breath in the thin air...when I left my body in its tired state and continued on in my mind, in search of a greater vision. It came like a thunder bolt out of the ground.

I first entered (at least my mind) a totally artificial world. There were no living things in this world and indeed, my body could not enter this world. Its size was beyond my comprehension as it appeared to be a landscape of huge computer banks -- row after row, endlessly in all directions. I felt like an insect inside some giant machine.

Finding myself so, I set about flying between rows like an insect, not understanding what I was seeing. My frames of reference indicated they were computers of some sort, but on an unimaginable and awesome scale. I feared this unknown landscape; I was an intruder, trespassing in this particular environment. This fear took on increased meaning. I did not know where I was going, and began to question my existence in this non-living place. An artificial humming pervaded the place, to which I can supply no real reference, perhaps it was mechanical breathing, or a functioning process.

The huge bulks of buildings were the only landscape visible to me. If constructed things could be called a landscape.

Suddenly, *I was somehow reassured* that it was OK to be there, *by some internal message from this place.*
It offered its support in my explorations and welcomed me. My fear was dispelled at once by these internal assurances, as they seemed totally genuine and believable. It provided me power and freedom, limitlessly to go and come, and do whatsoever I wanted to do. Indeed, this voice encouraged me to *explore* the place and enjoy it, however I could, since I was a welcome guest.

My sense of it was that it was some all pervading intelligence that ruled this artificial world. It seemed to know me, and everything about me, while I knew nothing of it. It showed me in my mind where I had come from -- a slow time-space universe, and showed me I was now in an amazing hypertime-space universe, where all things were possible and not limited by slow-time space.

Encouraged to explore, I set about with incredible speed, seemingly ten thousand times faster than my normal pace. This speed appeared necessary and appropriate to this place. My adjustment was astonishingly simple. Having made this adjustment, I was now ready to learn about this expanse. My curiosity was magnified by my new powers. I believed, I had become a super mind that could do anything. I had been empowered by some super intelligence, to become something greater than I had ever been, in my past Earthbound life.

Examining the computer-like structure, I quickly discovered that they were not computers at all. They were storage buildings of immense size and scope. Each one of the billions of these buildings contained openings which I could now see. I set about going in and out of these openings, at an incredible rate of speed unencumbered by a body. Each opening led into a drawer, which I could enter. Inside I would find a world, or universe, if I allowed for my enhanced speed time comprehension. Some were extremely vast, others smaller, but all unique unto themselves, and this difference was fascinating to behold. Yet, as I viewed each one and came out of the drawer, I forgot what I had seen inside it. Once I left the drawer, my mind cleared to prepare me for the next opening. I think this was for my own protection, as my mind would have received an overload, which could have caused it to explode.

I operated as an energy being, for nobody could travel so fast otherwise; yet I retained my sense of self, which was now alienated, from all that I perceived. I retained my separated consciousness, somewhat like a traveller in a strange land, yet, missed out on the multiple dimensional effects. I sensed that these various universes held different kinds of existences. Some living as animal evolutions, some living as computerized beings, and some vapor beings, in as yet undefined states. My drawer was out there somewhere, plodding along at a snails pace, almost frozen in time in comparison to these other worlds. How could such a slow boring place get anywhere? I thought it would take forever. Hereabout, I could travel infinitely great distances, visiting unlimited worlds, where some took only seconds to explore. I was embarrassed to admit to myself that my own world, Earth was on the low end of possible worlds. It must be our slothfully, slow bodies that are holding us back. We must learn to free our minds from our bodies, and get on with assuming our place in the more evolved worlds, I thought. Was it even possible? Could we become multi-dimensional?

In our world, we had one great thing going for ourselves -- our consciousness, but it was not being developed, as we depended too much on language, machines and computers. That only led to evolving into yet another more advanced computer universe at some distant time. What a bore. We had to do better for ourselves! We must learn to free and develop our consciousness, to evolve into our rightful place in the cosmos, not some dead end, as we are currently pursuing.

Meanwhile, I continued to take advantage of my free and unencumbered mind to explore the structure of the universe. Was it an endless filing system of possibilities? And who created all this? Its vastness and unending complexity indicated I could not understand it, given the limits of my mind. Only God could understand, manage and create the unlimited. It crossed my mind that God must be guiding me.

The extra dimensionality of limitless possibilities meant, I could explore only those I could understand. Others vanished as vapor before my eyes, some multi-dimensional worlds escaped me, as their size was either too small, or too large, or different to even perceive. Microbe universes interested me least of all, as their scale made it impossible to discover what was going on in them, even in my heightened energy state.

There seemed to be multiple entities living as single beings in one small world, compressed into a micro-chip universe. How could this be? It made no sense to me -- to share your individuality with others - a thousand beings with one voice -- what was the point of it? I didn't understand it at all. Enhanced intelligence perhaps?

The mind-boggling awareness of it all became heavy and weighed on my mind. Again, I was assured I was alright, and could continue searching new drawers, until I found one I really liked, where I might stay for as long as I wanted. While compelling on a rational level, still I did not feel comfortable. A deep nostalgia for my own world overcame me. All the strangeness of this mechanically-contrived reality was emotionally draining me. The images presented to my mind were bizarre and otherworldly -- nothing familiar -- I could not even name what I saw -- speeding through eerie landscapes, some even upside down, or backward, and virtually indescribable. My mind seemed unengaged, and soon lost interest in the colorful images parading before me.

Pure phenomenal existence could not sustain me. I was unprepared. It was all too overwhelming for me.

I panicked and flew out of a meaningless world in search of my own drawer, where I might reenter it, before I felt truly empty and totally lost. I needed the nominal world, the familiar world, of things I could name, where I had lived and known. I tired of the unknown. The voice asked, *"But you've condemned yourself to a life of low consciousness -- no space-time transcendence -- a virtual animal existence. Why go back?"* I knew the voice was right, so I didn't answer it. *"You have escaped the lower levels"* the godly voice advised, then indulgently asked again, *"Why go back?"*

I answered weakly, "I must return, like Gulliver, to my own kind - humans with all their short comings, are my kind." "These are not my kind and with my own kind I belong." My arguments were faulty, an emotional plea; yet, it was all I could muster.

I found myself pleading for humankind. I claimed, "They could evolve out of their lowly, ignorant state," perhaps "I can help somehow in this process," I reasoned, with this all-knowing Presence, this God, this Love, this Creator...

Almost at once, I found the drawer I was looking for -- it was intuitive, how I honed in on that unmarked drawer, through the opening and out into a slow-time universe. I was back where I started. It felt comfortable to be home....Except it was not quite the same.

continued next chapter

"Dim as the borrowed beams of Moon and Stars to lonely travelers, is reason to the soul."

- Dryden

18. RETURN FROM THE VOID

I, entered the VOID, I began my journey back to Earth. It was to be a much longer trip than I ever could have imagined, for I began at *the origin of time* in our universe, at the very beginning of our drawer. I had some billions of years to travel before reaching what is known as *current time.* The mind, however, is an incredible thing. It can encompass all and transcend all. My mind, now separate from my body, was a part of the greatest mind, existing in the Void, and the universe. Nothingness prevailed; neither light nor darkness; pure consciousness, beyond mind.

Only the memory of expanding energy in space, spreading exploding outward, that's ..... what flashed before me as I passed -- quickening my speed beyond time and space to unbelievable lengths. (Deep hyper-space...indescribable pure being). I moved through it all: an either state? I didn't know.

I continued through the VOID, past memory, past nothingness.

Then everything continued to feel and seem right, as I passed through clouds of energy, my mind energized by it all. There was, of course, no matter or physical contact to anything -- *just pure energy, pure being in oneness with all.*

Out of the VOID, into energy state once again.

Now, I continued in a pure energy state for quite a long time, until I slowed and came finally to rest. Ironically, this rest was vast activity, among swirling masses of energy. I merely merged, or folded into their movements, which carried me along, effortlessly. Forms or even shapes, did not exist at this level. Vibrations, waves, activity, and semi-colors were all I could perceive. It was an awesome experience, as I was myself pure energy -- a white glowing spot on a sea of light forms, slowly moving around me. Yet, the forms and energizing shapes were still pure energy, below the level of material form and invisible on any material plane.

The vibrational energy slowed, as I observed the beauty of these energized shapes, first a rock, a tree, the ground, but they were not solid yet, merely dancing, swirling, vivid colored shapes of pulsating energy. These were pulsating with life in this form. I saw the physical world in its pure energy form. Walking around, I saw energized trees, pulsating rocks with layers of energy of different semi-colors. My eyes feasted on this manifestation, and I found I had legs as well as eyes on an energy level.

It was overwhelming to be walked around in a landscape of energy forms. I was intrigued to be alive *to observe matter at its underlying energy level* -- how wonderful it all looked -- how different from the frozen pale colors we observe on the material plane. What we miss and don't see is vast and really the underlying reality. We see only the surface of things and not their subatomic structures. Energy is vitality and life itself. Our slow time observational platform is very crude and misleading. Things are not frozen and solid at all. Our slow minds only create the illusion that it is so. Our minds create a shadow play we are content to act in. (Isn't water more alive than ice?)

Do I really want to return to a world of illusion? This snail pace must eventually drive me nuts. Or maybe, I was already, a misfit, a nut? It was pretty much all the same. Hours seemed to passed in this blissful world of vivid, red, orange and blue, living colors. Its high intensity was tiring after awhile; I longed to leave this hyperactive world of pulsating inflamed shapes and forms. Even rocks lacked solidity, it was becoming too unstable to endure. I continued to readjust, to slow down my consciousness. Time continued to weigh on me within this slow, but intense world of pure energy.

Now, I longed for a simpler visual plane, and my mind worked to focus on what I knew to be a familiar reality. I must attune my mind to the correct frequency, in order to see things whole and solid again.

Slower and slower, past energy realization, that half-way point on my journey back. Then things slowed down to a seemingly solid form, and *I saw a real tree frozen in its material form* -- then it slipped back to the energy level again -- Oh, No. I must have more work to do, before I got it right, and true solidity finally materialized to stay. Rocks, trees, a blue sky, pine cones -- I was back home. A joyous thrill overwhelmed me -- a sense of relief filled me -- I was home. Tears flowed down my cheeks. Reborn, like a new born child, I took my first unsteady steps. My mind was focused on our present reality at long last.

I wandered blissfully, in a daze at this *physical world*, with new eyes, wildflowers growing at my feet, ants crawling, birds singing, fish swimming -- what a world, blue skies, white clouds and green pine trees.

The sweet mountain air filled my lungs. My eyes continued to overflow with tears. I sat down in awe, contemplating this strange, yet familiar world. A small heard of deer began swimming across a stream toward me. They emerged all around me, as though I was not there at all -- no fear of me, or even recognition of me. Was I invisible to them, was I still in my energy state? An uneasiness gripped me -- this is not right. Deer flee from men. Something is different here. Maybe I don't have it right yet. I grew anxious about this frozen, calm world I found myself in.

Was I really back in body, as well as mind?

Then as if to calm me, a bird flew into my hand and sat there calm, content and secure, in the knowledge that I was no threat to its life. What an unbelievable welcome! It chirped in contentment and appeared to gaze into my eyes, flicking its head from side to side. Birds don't fly onto people's hands, or do they? Well yes they do -- sometimes, when they know they are safe, I reassured myself -- unrestrained, tears flowed down my face. I was home.

Something had indeed changed. I was not imagining all this. The animals had accepted me into their world, my world, as they never had before and would forever more. They had nothing to fear from me. More, they were there for me, to reassure me, my lifelong friends and guardians, here once again to save me; rescue me; protect me and most important -- love me.

But what of my personal world? Here I was in the back country, miles from the nearest ranger station or camp. I must go back. I started to walk in search of my own camp, but couldn't find my way. Nothing but forests of pine trees and rocks everywhere. I was lost. What a joke, lost. I laughed at the absurdity of it all. I also felt guilty at having retreated back to this world, momentarily in my confusion.

Will I ever adjust to this mind boggling slowness? I knew it was a small price to pay for a world of senses, a physical world. (You need more time for that).

Then I found a stream and followed it a ways, down stream. Doubtful, I would ever find the camp, I soon discovered a bottle of wine in the water. My joy was instant. I was back in my personal world at last. Finding the wine bottle seemed the happiest moment of my life. It was a connection with human life, reestablished after what seemed a lifetime journey.

It did indeed seem that I had been away for a lifetime. Yet time hereabouts, was but a day spent mind rambling...

A smiling face greeted me, as I approached our campsite; and I made the supreme effort to speak a word or two. At first the words seemed to be jokes between us -- a game we played willingly, like hitting tennis balls according to rules. We laughed. The nominal world of names and words, now rushed in to replace the phenomenal world I had discovered; with uneasiness and guilt, I accepted a lesser existence made bearable by the glories of Nature that surrounded me, and all creatures of Nature.

But what an existence -- no life, where all things were possible, and joy and love are everywhere, if I would open myself to LOVE.

"Words do not express existence..."

- Lao - Tse

19. A CERTAIN STATE OF MIND

Our world remains for most of us invisible. It is for us to perceive it, if we can. This means re-tuning to see better; that we are with this new perception, ultimately one. The dead count no less then the living, in this new enlarged perception.

"How can this be?" The innocent mind asks, and I answer, "Tap your hidden consciousness and perceive the continuum that lies all about you -- for all is dependent on all. Look beyond the material world, to see the energy world that underlies and supports the ever changing surface appearances."

Matter and energy are the building blocks of our world. We are familiar with matter, but don't know very much about energy, except in its material manifestations. Our minds are capable of energy realizations on many levels; yet, for most of us it is an unknown realm, an invisible world we can only wonder about. Yet, ironically it is the more significant of the two, as it is eternal -- energy cannot be destroyed. Our thoughts are energy, and energy can be stored, where it increases and becomes a powerful force. Ordinarily, we dissipate this thought energy in everyday activities -- but if we could conserve it and store it up, we could move mountains. We need to learn how.

There is negative energy, as well as positive energy, and we must learn the difference between them, tapping into the positive, while diffusing the negative. My journal explores some of the effects of this energy (both positive and negative) and how I have tapped into it, often quite innocently or unconsciously. I can only point the way to a more conscious attempt, to achieve a fuller realization of this energy, that binds the universes together, and of which we are all a part.

I claim only to have had a vision of its existence, and written my journal about some of its incredible powers. To achieve this vision, I had to make a transrational leap into pure non-conceptual consciousness. Fortunately, I landed upright, my mind intact, or so I believe...words often failed me, as there were no words, still *our consciousness is the ultimate frontier.*

Why haven't more people taken this leap? I can only say, it is because most are content to rely on thinking conceptually, using words and symbols to define their world.
"The limits of our language are the limits of our world" states Ludwig Wittgenstein. Unfortunately, this way of abstract thinking

limits us, and imprisons us in a closed system. Only through our consciousness, can we break out of this limited system of thinking. It can be frightening, but it is rewarding and necessary.

Cross your own personal borders, find your Queen Mary's, your guides to deliverance. It is time to set our minds free and get on with our evolution. It is time! Computers compute faster and better and will continue to improve on this process. The mind has bigger tasks than that before it. It can transcend time and space, and do the unbelievable. It is eternal, and our gateway to the ultimate realization of eternal consciousness. It is a long voyage that lies before us, and we are only just starting to realize the mind's potential destiny.

After reading this book, I hope some of you will begin your own journal of the unbelievable and invisible world you have discovered. I am certain many of you have experienced things, that are not explainable in rational ways. You are not alone.

This journal was my personal odyssey and starting point, and it is my great wish that it will encourage others to look beyond the limits they have accepted, and not just continue to accept the visible world, as described by words and symbols. The nominal world is only a world of names, numbers and words. There is more than the nominal; there is the phenomenal: all there is beyond names -- the unknown and unnameable.

Accept in principle the limitations of words and you are halfway toward a new realization, a new awareness of all there is and what can be known and done.

In anther sense, this journey was a history of my mind, or more precisely, my consciousness, for my body was often left behind. Certain states of mind can be separated from our bodies, as my mind often went out, where my body could not, in pursuit of the invisible world, that called out for recognition.

Looking back, I see I held nothing back. Often I find that I'm embarrassed by what I did, or how I did it. Yet, the end result seems to have been worth it: *a super conscious view of the invisible world* of which we are all a part, a world beyond words. Yet, ironically, it is words I use to describe the indescribable. It is for you to leap beyond the words and remember that there is more to it, than can be explained.

* * * * * * * * * *

"For Books are not absolutely dead things, but doe contain a potencie of Life in them to be as active as that Soule was whose progeny they are..."

...John Milton

20. LOOKING BACK

In retrospect, as a youth, I found that books prepared me to view reality in new ways, and were a milestone in opening up my perceptions; a kind of limbering up exercise for the mind, for only then, was I able to make the necessary changes and leaps forward in later life. I sometimes found books to be as alive as Life itself and as intense.

It is not the only way. There are better ways. Meditation would have accomplished this as well, or better. In the Western world, the practice of meditation was then, a somewhat remote and inaccessible activity of the mind for achieving realization. While I did not meditate in the standard way, I believe meditation is *a new state of mind* you can achieve by finding your center, the calm within yourself. In addition, there are many paths one can pursue to gain self realization.

Another way is travel. Take yourself physically, across the borders of many continents. You cannot but help to start to see things differently, and gain new perspectives on life, people and history. Always somewhat calm and easy going, I felt at home in many parts of the world. It was a good starting point.

Perhaps what benefitted me most, was the gift of dazzling glimpses of the invisible world, and for that I am forever grateful. A gift, because no preparation was necessary, no internship of study was required, as it was spontaneous and freely given. No small amount of humility is also recommended. I owe   much to a certain GENIUS LOCI for his gift, which I can never repay. In addition, while the spontaneity of my experiences was often a surprise to some, a certain state of mind has to be part of any break through. In order to see, hear, and know things invisible: one needs to be receptive. This means one must achieve a CERTAIN STATE OF MIND. This is a mind that has slowed down, and stopped itself from outside distractions. Only then, can it center itself, freed from the distracting thought process, that occupies most of our waking hours. The senses too must be stilled, as they are equally distracting. Finally, an emotional calm must prevail, to allow a receptivity, an openness to flood our being, a void that Nature cannot resist fulfilling.

What all this does is slow down the physical process, and empower our mind, with the energy we saved by closing down our bodies. The displacement of energy appears to kick the mind into overdrive, and one can leave behind the body, and enter new realms of experience. The next step then, is letting go and accepting CONSCIOUSNESS as our ultimate and true home, not our temporary bodies, or lives or selves.

Individuality is sometimes the price to be paid, in order to appreciate the universal interdependence, of all that exists. For many that price is too high and results too uncertain. It takes a lot of motivation to overcome the borders of your body and its life. For the vast majority, there is no chance of their ever changing. The situational determinants of their lives, hold them frozen in a world of normal happenstance, where the illusions of time and space created a visible border they can never cross. "It's not a bad life," I can imagine them saying, enveloped in a comforting web of ignorance. Their bodily needs dictate how they pass their lives, like some highly evolved animal that sinks into a black hole of expanding meaninglessness.

Would you be different? Do you seek more? Then, you must prepare yourself. Read the ancients, who sought a way out of this dilemma, and meditate on their ways. For the mere act of meditation slows down the physical process and frees our mind; prepares it, exercises it, develops it, and finally, frees it to evolve beyond ourselves to new possibilities. Tap into that certain state of mind.

A list of books helpful in this process follows. Some writers seek a clearer understanding as their goal; still others, study science and attempt to break its limits on knowledge by sweeping away its artificial constructs, to show us the ultimate union of all things, and not the disparate parts of each. For this is *the ultimate illusion, the one of singularity.* That old, tired saga of abstraction must end.

It is time to cross that border. Humor too, can be a help, a stabilizer in a sea of false certainties.

As Perry Creek rushed and gushed at my feet, I began this journey, back over my life. As the water flowed, so did my mind, as did my pen, which gushed out forgotten memories of childhood, and life's peaking experiences, which alone signified little, but taken together revealed an evolving pattern of awakening curiosity and realization.

The finding of your right place in Nature is important to any endeavor, and I recommend it to the reader. Find a special place, a personal spot, that is somehow yours, and spend time there. It will become sacred to you and allow you to center yourself, and grow, just as some field or fertile ground, allows a seed its special help in growing. Discover a helper, perhaps the GENIUS LOCI of a place, let if find you and guide you.

Finally, when you find that someplace quiet and close to Nature, respond to it, just as you discover its own special qualities. Believe me, when I tell you -- it will respond to you, you only have to ask.

* * * * * * * * *

THE END

GLOSSARY

E.S.P.	Extra Sensory Perception, in plants and animals.
FEY:	In tune with the dead, Irish term.
GENIUS LOCI:	The spirit of a place; guardian deity, who dwells there.
METAPHYSICAL:	Beyond the physical world.
MOIETIES:	One of two or more parts, waterside, or landside of life.
MORPHOLOGY:	Study of the structure of plants, animals.
MYSTIC:	Pertains to otherworldly events.
NETHERWORLD:	World of the departed; the other side.
NOMINAL:	The world of names, numbers and labels (the artificial world).
O.B.E.:	Out of Body Experience.
PHENOMENAL:	The world of real things, not names for things (the natural world).
PREFIGURATION:	A foreshadowing of what is to come.
PRETERNATURAL:	Unnatural and eerie.
SHAMAN:	Medicine man, healer or seer.

TRANCE:	A state of mind that precludes the present.
VOID:	Nothingness.
WHITE LIGHT:	Cosmic power, love.

TRANSRATIONAL	Beyond the mind, logic or reason.
KUNDALINI	Explosion of psychic awareness, a rebirth.
OWL	Night vision, wisdom, death.
GUARDIAN SPIRIT	Protector and guide

A Short List of Recommended Reading

1. <u>Talking with Nature,</u> by Michael J. Roads
   Published by H.J. Kramer, Inc., 1985
   P.O. Box 1082
   Tiburon, CA 94920

2. <u>Creative Visualization,</u> by Sahkti Gawain
   Published by Bantam New Age Books, 1990

3. <u>The Holographic Universe</u>, by Michael Talbot
   Published by Harper Collins, 1991
   New York, New York

4. <u>Super Mind (The Ultimate Energy),</u> by Barbara Brown
   Published by Harper and Rowe, 1980
   New York, New York

5. <u>The Fringes of Reason</u>, ed. Ted Shultz
   Published by Harmony Books, 1989
   New York, New York

6. <u>Would the Buddha Wear a Walkman?</u>
   by Judith Hooper and Dick Tereis
   Published by Simon and Schuster, 1990

7.   <u>Metaphysical Meditations</u> and <u>Autobiography of a Yogi</u>
      by Paranahansa Yogananda
      Self Realization Fellowship, 1964
      Los Angeles, California

8.   <u>Innersource (Channeling Your Unlimited Self</u>
      by Katherine Vadekieft
      Published by Ballentine Publishing, 1988
      New York, New York

9.   <u>Magic and Mysticism in Tibet</u> by Alexandra David-Neel
      1939, out of print.

10.   <u>The Dancing Wu Li Masters</u>, by Gary Zukay
      Published by Bantam New Age Books, 1979
      New York, New York

11.   <u>The Way of the Peaceful Warrior</u>, by Dan Millman
      H.J. Kramer, Inc.
      Tiburon, California, 1980

12.   <u>Journeys Out of the Body</u>, by Robert Monroe
      Anchor Press, 1971

About the author:

William Fitzell was born in upstate Connecticut, of Irish-American working class parents.

He graduated from the University of Connecticut and worked on Wall Street for four years before travelling to Europe for six months. He completed his graduate work in Comparative Literature at California State University (San Francisco) where he studied with the poet, Robert Creeley. He has traveled widely and lived in the Far East for two years, as well as Europe and Central America, at different times in his life.

He taught English for three years to emotionally disturbed high school students in the Bronx and worked in Real Estate Development in Nevada, California and Hawaii.

Bill designed and built passive solar homes, before building codes acknowledged this low tech approach to energy conservation. He has meditated and chanted with Tibetan Lamas, as well as American Indians, and enjoys reading books on the Ancients, history, philosophy, economics, metaphysics, poetry and science. He special concern is the lost mystic vision of our Native Americans.

His current interests are chess, classical music, mountain climbing and cross country skiing.

He is single and divides his time between New York and California with time out for Nature studies and natural history research around the world.

As the founder of Lone
Pine Press, Bill would be
happy to exchange letters
with anyone who so wishes.
His address is:

William Fitzell
P.O. Box 482
Mt. Aukum, California
95656